PROSPERO'S CELL
and
REFLECTIONS ON A MARINE VENUS

by Lawrence Durrell

PROSPERO'S CELL
AND
REFLECTIONS
ON A
MARINE VENUS

BY
LAWRENCE DURRELL

A Dutton  *Paperback*

ILLUSTRATED

NEW YORK
E. P. DUTTON & CO., INC.

PROSPERO'S CELL

*A guide to the landscape
and manners of the island of
Corcyra*

by

LAWRENCE DURRELL

LAWRENCE DURRELL, a British citizen of Irish parentage, was born in the Himalaya region of India. His first ten years were spent in India. After schooling in England, he decided to become a writer. Throughout the 1930's Mr. Durrell devoted most of his talents to his poetry which has won much acclaim. His first novel, *The Black Book*, was published in Paris in 1938, and was cited by T. S. Eliot as being one of the great hopes for modern English fiction. *The Black Book* was published in the United States for the first time in 1960.

World War II temporarily interrupted Mr. Durrell's literary career. During the war years and for some time thereafter, he served Great Britain in various official and diplomatic capacities in Athens, Cairo, Rhodes and Belgrade.

The publication of *Justine* in 1957, and the subsequent appearance of *Balthazar* (1958), *Mountolive* (1959), and *Clea* (1960) as parts of the same magnificent series called "The Alexandria Quartet" devoted to an examination of the various aspects of love, immediately caused Mr. Durrell to be recognized as one of the greatest and most important writers of modern times.

PROSPERO'S CELL *and* REFLECTIONS ON A MARINE VENUS were first published together in one volume in 1960.

Acknowledgements

Acknowledgements for material used in this book must be made to:

Dr. Theodore Stephanides, R.A.M.C., who has placed five unpublished monographs at my disposal containing the fruits of ten years' research; Mr. Jean Tricoglou of Cairo for illustrations and other matter; Mr. Theodore Moschonas for valuable suggestions; and to Miss Y. Cohen for invaluable aid in copying out manuscripts.

FOUR
OF THE CHARACTERS
IN THIS BOOK
ARE REAL PEOPLE
AND APPEAR HERE
BY THEIR OWN CONSENT.
TO THE FOUR OF THEM
THEODORE STEPHANIDES
ZARIAN
THE COUNT D.
AND MAX NIMIEC
IT IS DEDICATED BY THE AUTHOR
IN LOVE AND ADMIRATION

'A Greekish isle, and the most pleasant place that ever our eyes beheld for the exercise of a solitary and contemplative life. . . . In our travels many times, falling into dangers and unpleasant places, this only island would be the place where we would wish ourselves to end our lives.'—ANTHONY SHERLEY, *His Persian Adventure 1601*.

Contents

Illustrations

Prospero's Cell

I

Divisions upon Greek Ground

'No tongue: all eyes: be silent.'
The Tempest

Somewhere between Calabria and Corfu the blue really begins. All the way across Italy you find yourself moving through a landscape severely domesticated—each valley laid out after the architect's pattern, brilliantly lighted, human. But once you strike out from the flat and desolate Calabrian mainland towards the sea, you are aware of a change in the heart of things: aware of the horizon beginning to stain at the rim of the world: aware of *islands* coming out of the darkness to meet you.

In the morning you wake to the taste of snow on the air, and climbing the companion-ladder, suddenly enter the penumbra of shadow cast by the Albanian mountains—each wearing its cracked crown of snow—desolate and repudiating stone.

A peninsula nipped off while red hot and allowed to cool into an antarctica of lava. You are aware not so much of a landscape coming to meet you invisibly over those blue miles of water as of a climate. You enter Greece as one might enter a dark crystal; the form of things becomes irregular, refracted. Mirages suddenly swallow islands, and wherever you look the trembling curtain of the atmosphere deceives.

Other countries may offer you discoveries in manners or lore or landscape; Greece offers you something harder—the discovery of yourself.

10.4.37

It is a sophism to imagine that there is any strict dividing line between the waking world and the world of dreams. N. and I, for example, are confused by the sense of several contemporaneous lives being lived inside us; the sensation of being mere points of reference for space and time. We have chosen Corcyra perhaps because it is an ante-room to Aegean Greece with its smoke-grey volcanic turtle-backs lying low against the ceiling of heaven. Corcyra is all Venetian blue and gold—and utterly spoilt by the sun. Its richness cloys and enervates. The southern valleys are painted out boldly in heavy brush-strokes of yellow and red while the Judas trees punctuate the roads with their dusty purple explosions. Everywhere you go you can lie down on grass; and even the bare northern reaches of the island are rich in olives and mineral springs.

25.4.37

The architecture of the town is Venetian; the houses above the old port are built up elegantly into slim tiers with narrow alleys and colonnades running between them; red, yellow, pink, umber— a jumble of pastel shades which the moonlight transforms into a dazzling white city built for a wedding cake. There are other curiosities; the remains of a Venetian aristocracy living in over-grown baronial mansions, buried deep in the country and sur-rounded by cypresses. A patron saint of great antiquity who lies, clad in beautifully embroidered slippers, in a great silver casket, apt for the performance of miracles.

29.4.37

It is April and we have taken an old fisherman's house in the extreme north of the island—Kalamai. Ten sea-miles from the town, and some thirty kilometres by road, it offers all the charms of seclusion. A white house set like a dice on a rock already vener-able with the scars of wind and water. The hill runs clear up into the sky behind it, so that the cypresses and olives overhang this room in which I sit and write. We are upon a bare promontory with its beautiful clean surface of metamorphic stone covered in olive and ilex: in the shape of a *mons pubis*. This is become our unregretted home. A world. Corcyra.

5.5.37

The books have arrived by water. Confusion, adjectives, smoke, and the deafening pumping of the wheezy Diesel engine. Then the caique staggered off in the direction of St. Stephano and the Forty Saints, where the crew will gorge themselves on melons and fall asleep in their coarse woollen vests, one on top of the other, like a litter of cats, under the ikon of St. Spiridion of Holy Memory. We are depending upon this daily caique for our provisions.

6.5.37

Climb to Vigla in the time of cherries and look down. You will see that the island lies against the mainland roughly in the form of a sickle. On the landward side you have a great bay, noble and serene, and almost completely landlocked. Northward the tip of the sickle almost touches Albania and here the troubled blue of the Ionian is sucked harshly between ribs of limestone and spits of sand. Kalamai fronts the Albanian foothills, and into it the water races as into a swimming-pool: a milky ferocious green when the north wind curdles it.

7.5.37

The cape opposite is bald; a wilderness of rock-thistle and melancholy asphodel—the drear sea-squill. It was on a ringing spring day that we discovered the house. The sky lay in a heroic blue arc as we came down the stone ladder. I remember N. saying distinctly to Theodore: 'But the quietness alone makes it another country.' We looked through the hanging screen of olive-branches on to the white sea wall with fishing-tackle drying on it. A neglected balcony. The floors were cold. Fowls clucked softly in the gloom where the great olive-press lay, waiting its season. A cypress stood motionless—as if at the gates of the underworld. We shivered and sat on the white rock to eat, looking down at our own faces in the motionless sea. You will think it strange to have come all the way from England to this fine Grecian promontory where our only company can be rock, air, sky—and all the elementals. In letters home N. says we have been cultivating the tragic sense. There is no explanation. It is enough to record that everything is exactly as the fortune-teller said it would be. White house, white rock, friends, and a narrow style of loving: and perhaps a book which will grow out of these scraps, as from the rubbish of these old

Divisions upon Greek Ground

Venetian tombs the cypress cracks the slabs at last and rises up fresh and green.

9.5.37

We are lucky in our friends. Two of them seem of almost mythological quality—Ivan Zarian and the arcane professor of broken bones Theodore Stephanides. Zarian is grey, eminent and imposing with his mane of hair and his habit of conducting himself as he intones his latest love-song; he claims to be Armenia's greatest poet with a firmness and modesty that completely charm. He has spent nearly two years here intoning his work to anyone who would listen, and making an exhaustive study of the island wines. He has managed to convert the top floor of the St. George Hotel into a workroom—indeed a wilderness of manuscript and paintings. Here, looking out upon the blunt fortifications of the Eastern Fort, and pausing from time to time to relish a glass of wine, he compiles his literary column for some new world Armenian newspapers. On Friday, the 8th of March, he sent me a friendly message reading:

> Dear Durrell: we miss you but most your beautiful wife. Dear, boy, yes, certainly I have immortalized you this week. I have written this epoch of our lives. Great love from Zarian.

Zarian walks as if he wears a heavy cloak. A copious and extravagant figure it was he who instituted our literary meetings once a week at the 'Sign of the Partridge', off the main square of the town. Zarian possesses an extraordinary typewriter which enables him, by simply revolving the bed of type, to write in French and Italian as well as in Armenian and Russian. At these weekly meetings he rises to his feet and, in a beautifully controlled voice, recites the 'to be or not to be' speech from Hamlet, first in French, and then in Armenian, Russian, Italian, German and Spanish. He scorns to learn English properly.

From my notebook   *12.5.37*

For Theodore's portrait: fine head and golden beard: very Edwardian face—and perfect manners of Edwardian professor.

Divisions upon Greek Ground

Probably reincarnation of comic professor invented by Edward Lear during his stay in Corcyra. Tremendous shyness and diffidence. Incredibly erudite in everything concerning the island. Firm Venezelist, and possessor of the dryest and most fastidious style of exposition ever seen. Thumbnail portrait of bearded man in boots and cape, with massive bug-hunting apparatus on his back stalking across country to a delectable pond where his microscopic world of algae and diatoms (the only real world for him) lies waiting to be explored. Theodore is always being arrested as a foreign agent because of the golden beard, strong English accent in Greek, and mysterious array of vessels and swabs and tubes dangling about his person. On his first visit to Kalamai house he had hardly shaken hands when sudden light came into his eye. Taking a conical box from his pocket he said 'excuse me' with considerable suppressed excitement and advanced to the drawing-room wall to capture a sand-fly exclaiming as he did so in a small triumphant voice 'Got it. Four hundred and second.'

17.5.37

Gulls turning down wind; to-day a breath of sirocco and the sea grinding and crushing up its colours under the house; the town gardens steaming in their rotten richness. The Duchess of B. abroad in a large hat, riding in a horse-carriage. Shuttered mansions with the umbrella pines rapping at the windows. On the great southern shelf you can see the road running white as a scar against the emerald lake; the olives are tacking madly from grey to silver, and behind the house the young cypresses are like drawn bows. Nicholas who was standing firm and square before us on the jetty a minute ago is now that speck of red sail against the mountains. Then at night it dies down suddenly and the colour washes back into the sky. At the 'Sign of the Partridge' Zarian gives a discourse on landscape as a form of metaphysics. 'The divine Plato said once that in Greece you see God with his compasses and dividers.' N. maintains Lawrence's grasp of place against an English boy who declares all the Lawrentian landscapes to be invented not described; while Theodore surprises by asking in a small voice for a glass of wine (he does not drink) and adding in an even smaller voice: 'What is causality?'

Divisions upon Greek Ground

Causality is this dividing floor which falls away each morning when I am back on the warm rocks, lying with my face less than a foot above the dark Ionian. All morning we lie under the red brick shrine to Saint Arsenius, dropping cherries into the pool—clear down two fathoms to the sandy floor where they loom like drops of blood. N. has been going in for them like an otter and bringing them up in her lips. The Shrine is our private bathing-pool; four puffs of cypress, deep clean-cut diving ledges above two fathoms of blue water, and a floor of clean pebbles. Once after a storm an ikon of the good Saint Arsenius was found here by a fisherman called Manoli, and he built the shrine out of red plaster as a house for it. The little lamp is always full of sweet oil now, for St. Arsenius guards our bathing.

At evening the blue waters of the lagoon invent moonlight and play it back in fountains of crystal on the white rocks and the deep balcony; into the high-ceilinged room where N.'s lazy pleasant paintings stare down from the walls. And invisibly the air (cool as the breath from the heart of a melon) pours over the window-sills and mingles with the scent of the exhausted lamps. It is so still that the voice of a man up there in the dusk under the olives disturbs and quickens one like the voice of conscience itself. Under the glacid surface of the sea fishes are moving like the suggestion of fishes—influences of curiosity and terror. And now the stars are shining down frostblown and taut upon this pure Euclidian surface. It is so still that we have dinner under the cypress tree to the light of a candle. And after it, while we are drinking coffee and eating grapes on the edge of the mirror a wind comes: and the whole of heaven stirs and trembles—a great branch of blossoms melting and swaying. Then as the candle draws breath and steadies everything hardens slowly back into the image of a world in water, so that Theodore can point into the water at our feet and show us the Pleiades burning.

At such moments we never speak; but I am aware of the brown

arms and throat in the candlelight and the brown toes in the sandals. I am aware of a hundred images at once and a hundred ways of dealing with them. The bowl of wild roses. The English knives and forks. Greek cigarettes. The battered and sea-stained notebook in which I rough out my poems. The rope and oar lying under the tree. The spilth of the olive-press which will be gathered for fuel. The pile of rough stone for the building of a garden wall. A bucket and an axe. The peasant crossing the orchard in her white head-dress. The restless cough of the goat in the barn. All these take shape and substance round this little yellow cone of flame in which N. is cutting the cheese and washing the grapes. A single candle burning upon a table between our happy selves.

4.6.37

I have preserved the text of Theodore's first communication. It arrived on Sunday by the evening boat and was delivered at the door by Spiro the village idiot. Since it was superscribed URGENT I made the messenger the gift of a drachma.

'*I learn with considerable joy from our mutual friend Z that you are intending a written history of the isle. It is a project which I myself have long contemplated but owing to the diffuseness of my interests and lack of literary talent I have always felt myself unequal to the task. I hasten however to place all my material at your service, and on Tuesday will send you (a) my synoptic history of the island, (b) my facts about St. Spiridion, (c) my fresh-water biology of Corcyra, (d) a short account of the geology of the island of Corcyra. This should interest you. It is only the beginning. Yours sincerely, Theodore Stephanides.*'

It is on the strength of this that I have entered into a correspondence characterized on my part by flights of deliberately false scholarship, and on his by the unsmiling and fastidious rectitude of a research worker. Our letters are carried to and fro by the island boats. It is, as he says, only a beginning.

7.6.37

At night the piper sometimes plays, while his grazing sheep walk upon the opposite cape and browse among the arbutus and scrub. We lie in bed with our skins rough and satiny from the salt and listen. The industrious and rather boring nightingales are abashed by the soft liquid quartertones, the unearthly quibbles of the flute. There is form without melody, and the notes are emptied as if drop by drop on to the silence. It is the wheedling voice of the sirens that Ulysses heard.

9.6.37

We have been betraying our origins. N. has decided to build a garden on the rock outside the house. We will have to bring the soil down in sacks, and employ the Aegean technique of walled boxes and columns. The design is N.'s and its execution is in the hands of John and Nicholas, father and son, who are the best masons in the village. The father builds slightly lopsided because, he says, he is blind in one eye; and his son comes silently behind him to rectify his errors and admire his facility in pruning the mountain stone into rough blocks. John is most comfortable squatting on his haunches in the shadow cast by his wide straw hat and talking scandal; he moves along the wall in a series of hops like a clipped magpie. His son is a fresh-faced dumb youth with a vivid smile and excellent manners. He dresses in the hideous cloth cap and torn breeches of the European workman, while his father still wears pointed slippers. It is worth perhaps recording the traditional island costume, now seldom seen except at festivals and dances.

Blue embroidered bolero jacket with black and gold braid and piping.
A white soft shirt with puffed sleeves.
Baggy blue breeches called Vrakes.
White woollen gaiters.
And pointed Turkish slippers with no pom-pom.
Either a soft red fez with a blue tassel
Or a white straw hat.

11.6.37

The straw from the packing-cases will go to cover the floor of the magazine where the goat is tethered. The rooms look lovely and gracious with their white-washed walls, and the few bright paintings and books. The windows give directly on to the sea, so that its perpetual sighing is the rhythm of our work and our sleeping. By day it runs golden on the ceilings, reflecting back the bright peasant rugs—a ship, a gorgon, a loom, a cypress-tree; reflecting back the warm crude pottery of our table; reflecting back N. now brown-skinned and blonde, reading in a chair with her legs tucked under her. Calm eyes, calm hair, and clear white teeth like those of a young carnivore. As Father Nicholas says: 'What more does a man want than an olive-tree, a native island, and woman from his own place?'

13.6.37

The man and his wife are fine creatures. He is called Anastasius and she Helen. It is obvious from their children that the marriage was a marriage of love rather than convenience. She is most delicately formed in a deep silken olive-colour; their hair has that deep black which shines out in sudden hints of blue—the simile of the Klepthic poems says 'hair like the wing of a raven'. Beautifully formed eyebrows above their dark eyes, clear and circumflex. Only their hands and feet—like those of all peasants—are blunt and hideous: mere spades grown upon the members through a long battle with soil, ropes, and wood. Their daughters are called Sky and Freedom.

17.6.37

'Formal geology', writes Theodore in his treatise, 'will still find features of interest in Corcyra; and if the form of the island in general is conditioned by its limestone features, there are many interesting configurations worth the mature attention of field-workers.'

Southward the land falls gently away to the white cape, luxuriant and steaming; every curve here is a caress, a nakedness to the delighted eyes, an endearment. Every prospect is contained in a frame of cypress and olives and brilliant roofs. Inlets, lakes, islands lead one slowly down to the deserted salt-pans beyond Lefkimi.

Two great ribs of mountain enclose this Eden. One runs from north to south along the western ranges; while from east to west the dead lands rise sheer to Pantocrator. It is in the shadow of this mountain that we live. Here little vegetation clings to the rock; water, harsh with the taste of iron and ice cold, runs from the ravines; the olive-trees are stunted and contorted in an effort to maintain a purchase on this crumbling gypsum territory. Their roots, like the muscles of wrestlers, hang from the culverts. Here the peasant girls lounge on the hillside—flash of colour like a bird —with a flower between their teeth, while their goats munch the tough thistle and ilex.

'All epochs from the Jurassic are represented here. In the north the configurations of certain caves suggest volcanic origins, but this has not yet been proved.' The grottoes at Paleocastrizza are ribbed with jewels which smoulder purple and yellow and nacre in the reflected light of the intruding sea. Grapes from this mountain region yield a wine that bubbles ever so slightly; an undertone of sulphur and rock. Ask for red wine at Lakones and they will bring you a glass of volcano's blood.

20.6.37

Zarian sends me a poem about the island in Armenian to which he adds an English translation. Writing of Corcyra he says: 'The gold and moving blue have stained our thoughts so that the darkness is opaque, and we see in our dreams the world as if in some great Aquarium. Exiles and sharers, we have found a new love. This is Corcyra, the chimney-corner of the world.'

Since I have nothing else I reciprocate with my poem on Manoli, the landscape painter of Greece: 'After a lifetime of writing acrostics he took up a brush and everything became twice as attentive. Trees had been simply trees before. Distinctions had been in ideas. Now the old man went mad, for everything undressed and ran laughing into his arms.'

Theodore promises 'Maps, Tables, and Statistics'. I am making no attempt to control all this material. If I wrote a book about Corcyra it would not be a history but a poem.

World of black cherries, sails, dust, arbutus, fishes and letters from home.

24.6.37

Fragment from a novel about Corcyra which I began and destroyed: 'She comes down through the cloud of almond-trees like a sentence of death, all dressed in white and leading her flock to the very gates of the underworld. Our hearts melt in us at the candour of her smile and the beauty of her walk. Soon she is to marry Niko, the fat moneylender, and become a stout shrew drudging out to olive-pickings on a lame donkey, smelling of garlic and animal droppings.'

25.6.37

N. has been away for three days in the town, trying to buy a few odds and ends of furnishings for the house. The silence here is like a discernible pulse—the heart-beat of time itself. I am all day alone on the great rock; the sea is cold—its chill hurts the back of the throat like an iced wine; but blue as the grave, while the sun is blazing. To-night a letter by boat from her. 'I have bought us a twenty-foot cutter, carvel built, and Bermuda rigged. I am terribly excited—the whole world seems to be open before us. But O how wine-darkly she rides. Bringing her out to-morrow with Petros. Wait for me at the point.'

26.6.37

The problem of water for the garden is serious. The only spring is on the highroad a quarter of a mile up the ravine. All our water is carried down on the backs of womenfolk in huge earthen jars. We had Nick the douser down with his hazel-twig, but after walking backwards and forwards grumbling under his breath for a quarter of an hour, he pronounced the water 'too deep'—over five metres. As the house stands at sea-level we could not afford to dig and have the well turn brackish on us. It must be a mountain spring or nothing. Meanwhile my two erudites send their suggestions by water—each a model of its kind. Zarian suggests a machine that a friend of his invented for turning salt water into fresh; he forgets how it works but he will write to America at once for particulars. It costs rather a lot but would save trouble; we would simply put one end of the pump in the sea and spray the garden with fresh water. Theodore, on the other hand, suggests something more practical. In the droughty summer the natives of Macedonia construct themselves ice-boxes by pulping quantities of prickly pear which they bury in a hole to the depth of about two metres. The hole is filled with fine pebbles or stones, and when the rains come the absorbing pulp of the prickly pear sups up the water and retains it in its pores. He suggests that we should adopt this scheme for our walled garden-boxes. 'Be careful', he adds, 'to pulp the tree well. Count V. tried this in his country house garden on my advice but omitted to pulp the prickly pear so that by some unfortunate chance he found it growing up through his flower-beds. This, as you can imagine, was a catastrophe and he has not spoken to me since.'

3·7·37

The conventions of our weekly meeting at 'The Partridge' are charming; we share our food, our criticism, and even our mail. When Zarian gets a letter from Unamuno or Celine it is read out and passed round the table; and when I get one of Henry Miller's rambling exuberant letters from Paris the company is delighted. This is the real island flavour; our existence here is in this delectable landscape, remote from the responsibilities of an active life in Europe, have given us this sense of detachment from the real world. Over the smoking copper pans the face of Paul, the Cretan manager of the tavern, looms strangely. He watches over the dishes, pausing to wipe the sweat out of his great brown moustaches; his manner is that of one who has dealt with epicures for a lifetime. Later Luke, the blind guitarist, arrives, led by his small son —a child of great beauty and pallor. Its face is the face of a Byzantine ikon. Stiffly the old red-faced man sits down on a chair, and strikes his instrument; the small expressionless face of the boy is cocked over his cheap violin as he tunes it. Then they strike up one of the familiar Greek jazz songs—inevitably a tango; yet the words haunt, and the refrain is taken up to the accompaniment of knife and fork by the roystering Zarian, Peltours the lean Russian painter, Veronica and John, Nimiec, Theodore. The narrow white-washed room with its ugly tables and cheap advertisements rings.

'Loneliness, Loneliness,
You are bitter company to us.'

Afterwards we walk down in the warm night to the dark slipway, and, as the moon is rising, shake out the jib of the *Van Norden*, start her engine, and put our noses northward into the night.

Divisions upon Greek Ground

Lights move on the darkness hardly grazing the surface of the consciousness. From the receding shore, clear on the water, we can hear Zarian still contending some majestic literary theme. N. curls in a rug and dips her grapes over the side in the shining sea. And hollow over the harbour, speeding us with the promise of a safe arrival, St. Spiridion strikes the hour of midnight.

4.7.37

We breakfast at sunrise after a bathe. Grapes and Hymettos honey, black coffee, eggs, and the light clear-tasting Papastratos cigarette. Unconscious transition from the balcony to the rock outside. Lazily we unhook the rowboat and make for the point where the still blue sea is twisted in a single fold—like a curtain caught by a passing hand. A shale beach, eaten out of the cliff-point, falling to a row of sunken rocks. A huge squat fig-tree poised like a crocodile on the edge of the water. Five fathoms directly off the point so that sitting here on this spit we can see the dolphins and the steamers passing within hail almost. We bathe naked, and the sun and water make our skins feel old and rough, like precious lace. Yesterday we found the foetus of an octopus, colourless ball of gelatine, which throbbed invisibly in the palm of the hand; to-day the fisherboys have found our beach. They have written Angli (*Ἄγγλοι*) in charcoal on one of the rocks, we have responded with 'Hellenes' which is fair enough. We have never seen them. N. draws a little head in a straw hat with a great nose and moustache.

5.7.37

Yesterday was a fisherman's holiday; first a great glistening turtle was washed up on the beach at the cliff edge. It was quite dead and its heavy yellow eyelids were drawn down over its eyes giving it a sinister and reptilian air of being half asleep. It must have weighed about as much as the dinghy. I expected the fishermen to make some use of the meat but nobody has touched it—except the village dogs which have been worrying its flippers.

More exciting was the killing of the eel. We were unhooking the boat when a small boy who was helping us cast off pointed to something in the water and exclaimed 'Zmyrna'. I was about to

Divisions upon Greek Ground

probe about with an oar—for I could see nothing in the shadow of the great rock—when Anastasius came running like a flash from the carpenter's shop. He held two heavy four-pronged tridents. For a moment or two he stared keenly down into the water; we could see nothing beyond the movements of marine life, the swaying of the seaweed fronds and the strange flickering passage of small fish. Then Anastasius lowered a piece of wood—simply the unshod shaft of a trident—into the darkest patch of the shadow. There was a small audible snap—as of a rat-trap closing—and his shoulders became rigid; maintaining his pressure on the wood he picked up a trident and lowering the point slowly into the water suddenly struck home at an angle. There was a sudden convulsion among the seaweed and the head of the eel emerged; it seemed to our terrified eyes about the size of a dog's head and infinitely more senseless and wicked. The trident had pierced the skull and while it was still dazed from the blow Anastasius strove to dislodge it from its perch. Help, too, was at hand. Old Father Nicholas came racing down with a couple of sharpened boat-hooks and these were driven into the meaty shoulders of the eel.

It took three of them to lug it on to the rock, and for a quarter of an hour on dry land it fought savagely, with two tridents piercing its brain and two more in its sides. I can hear the dry snapping of its jaws on the stick as I write. It had muscle on it like a wrestler, and its tail tapered into a great finned bolster of brown gristle—a turbine; altogether the whole fish looked more like an American invention than anything from the water-world; and it had the ferocity and determination of Satan. It was interesting to see how *afraid* its evil aspect made one; long after it was dead the peasants were driving their tridents into it with imprecations; and everyone gave it a wide berth until it stiffened with an unmistakable rigor.

Another reflection of this anxiety: Helen was given a terrific scolding because she was in the habit to poking about in the rocks at low tide barefooted. 'And if such an animal got you?' Anastasius kept repeating. 'And if such an animal got you?'

The children stood like carvings by the sea in their red flannel frocks, never taking their eyes off the dead eel. They all had their thumbs in their mouths. Then Sky removed her thumb with a

THE EASTERN ADRIATIC

*drawn by Bernard J. Palmer after a copy of a late Portolano engraved in Italy
by Lucini for Robert Dudley, 1646*

little sigh and said: 'Let's go,' and they trotted off up among the olive-trees.

To-night we shall have eel-meat with red sauce for supper.

6.7.37

At night the fishing-boats put out; they carry great carbide-flares to attract the fish to the nets, and the dark bulk of the Albanian shadow opposite is studded with their jewelled fires. Dark red and smoky, occasional fires glow on the hills themselves; yellow and small along the sealine shine the lights of the solitaries who hunt alone in boats with tridents. I must record the method and the instruments employed in carbide fishing—but to-night my mind is full of a story which Nicholas has been telling me. It concerns two lovers in Corcyra during the occupation of the Turks. He was an Albanian Moslem and she a Greek. During a political crisis he was banished from the island and she was kept guarded in a country-house on the coast; before he left they agreed to signal to each other by lighting fires—he on the tip of Cape Stiletto and she at Govino on the second Sunday of every month. For three years these fire-messages passed telling each of them that the other was well. Then one night the girl died and her attendants forgot to light the accustomed fire. The fire on the Cape, however, burned at the accustomed time. But when her Albanian lover saw no response to his message he knew that something serious was afoot and crossed over to the island to try and visit her. He was caught and murdered. Yet ever since then on the second Sunday of every month there is a fire alight on the end of Cape Stiletto; it burns brackishly for a few hours and then goes out. Sometimes it shows a greenish flame. It is *not* a carbide-fisher as there is no shallow beach off the cape; it is *not* a scrub-fire because on this bare promontory there is nothing but rock. It is, says Nicholas, the Albanian sending his message—a message to which there is never any answer, for Govino headland lies dark and unresponsive to the west, under the hump of shadow from the mountains.

7.7.37

The boat rides beautifully. N. has christened her the *Van Norden.* Now in the still weather we keep her anchored close under the

Divisions upon Greek Ground

balcony; she is smart in her black paint with brass fittings and a white awning. Yesterday we took her out in a fresh north-easterly wind up as far as the Forty Saints. I wanted to conquer my timidity about a following wind. But she ran before it like a knife. The wood around the lead keel however is puffed and cankered; she must come out and be painted against worms. I notice that we speak about her in the compassionate and familiar way that people speak about their pets. The young schoolmaster Niko is full of envy, and in order to show off we invited him for a sail in the evening. He handles her much more sensitively than either of us; with roughness and determination, with an unerring sense of what to ask her. She turns upwind like a dancer and falters into the still water under the house like a vessel of silk.

II

The Island Saint

The island is really the Saint: and the Saint is the island. Nearly all the male children are named after him. All the island craft carry his tintype—mournful of beard and brow—nailed to their masts of unseasoned cypress wood. To use his name in an oath is to bind yourself by the most solemn of vows, for St. Spiridion is still awake in Corcyra after nearly two thousand years on earth. He is the Influence of the island.

In the chapel of the church of his name he lies, looking a trifle misanthropic but determined, as befits one who has seen most sides of life on earth, and who is on equal terms with heaven. The sarcophagus is deeply lined and comfortable; he lies in hibernating stillness in his richly wrought casket, whose outer shell of silver is permanently clouded by the breath of the faithful who stoop to kiss it. The darkness swims with chalices and banners—all the garishness of Byzantine church-decoration. A style of art which is literal rather than figurative: the saint has a real nimbus of silver let into the canvas round his haunted oval face. Eyes of black olive stare unrepenting down from every wall.

Here in the church of St. Spiridion, Venice and Turkey compete in silver and brass, in bronze and iron; and under this tortured inlay-work and colour the dark pagan eyes still stare with their fleshly hunger—reminding you how close the old pantheon is, locked in this narrow ritualism.

Light, dammed up by the obtuse walls, bursts fiercely through the great porches and explodes like butter over the scarves and head-dresses, the beards and lips and clothes of the peasants.

The saint lies quite composed in his casket. He is a mummy, a small dried-up anatomy, whose tiny feet (clad in embroidered slippers) protrude from a vent at the bottom of his sarcophagus.

The Island Saint

If you are one of the faithful you may stoop and kiss his slippers. He will answer your prayers.

Who is Spiridion? His life is an amusing study in myth. He was born and lived as a shepherd in the mountains of Cyprus. When his wife died he buried his unhappiness between the four walls of a monastery, becoming immediately remarkable for his fineness of spirit and fidelity to God. As a bishop he took part in the great council of Nicea, where he gave miraculous testimony of the then disputed doctrine of the Trinity by casting a brick (which he must have secreted about his person) to the ground, where it immediately gushed fire and water in one.

A long life, many good works, and not a few miracles contributed to his subsequent popularity, so that when he died, this humble Bishop of Trymithion (he was well over ninety years old) had become revered almost as a saint.

He was buried: but the restless virtue in him could not waste in the earth—and now exhalations of sweetness from his coffin began to trouble the orthodox. A spray of red roses broke from his tomb —to-day still to be seen in Cyprus. These combined omens persuaded the religious to dig his body up—and no sooner was this done than Spiridion justified his resurrection by a miracle, entering, so to speak, into his posthumous life and career from the refuge of God Himself.

He had hardly a chance to settle down for when Cyprus fell to the Saracens his relics were removed to Constantinople; and when Constantinople itself was threatened by the locust hordes of the Moslem world he was once more forced to change his country of operations.

At this time the Saint was in private ownership. A Greek, recorded as having been both priest and wealthy citizen, and whose name survives as Kalocheiritis, preserved him equally against the unbelieving Moslems and incipient decomposition. This Greek appears to have had some traffic in saints since at the same time he possessed the embalmed body of another saint—a lady of virtue —Saint Theodora Augusta.

Kalocheiritis packed his two saints (very much as a pedlar packs his apparatus) in two shapeless sacks. He slung them, one on each side of his mule, and telling the curious that they contained animal fodder, crossed one fine spring morning into the enchanted land-scapes of Greece.

The long conversations held between Augusta and Spiridion as they jolted over the bare mountain tied in sacks, are not recorded by the hagiographers—and indeed have aroused the curiosity of none besides myself. I cannot believe however that such a long journey can have been passed without some exchange of theological pleasantries—though I do not claim the least gallantry or any such immodesty for Spiridion; but they could not have gone on together, day by day, roped like carrion in their stifling sacks, without feeling the necessity for speech. They must have smelt together the bruised rawness of the sage even above the clinical richness of the embalming fluids. The air must have sharpened as they reached the pine-belted slopes of the Epirus mountains; the incessant halts must have been intolerable to the dead man and woman, who had need of neither food nor sleep, but jolted on in darkness rich only in a knowledge of God.

Paramythia in Epirus gave them refuge until 1456 when they were brought across the blue waters of the gulf to Corcyra, and laid in the chapel of Michael the Archangel.

Here, it appears they decided to stay, the two saints. Perhaps the fecundity and beauty of the island appealed to them as much as the merry laziness of the natives. At all events here they have both withstood fire, siege and famine for several hundred years. When the Turks appeared with their menacing hordes it was the Saint who dispersed them disguised as a south-westerly squall; when epilepsy struck down the Armenian quarter it was Theodora who expelled it; and when the great plague of Naples selected Corcyra as a theatre of operations Spiridion is said to have sent it off to Naples with one contemptuous invocation, in the shape of a frightened black cat.

Owing to the rights of possession the Saint has passed through many hands. The three sons of Kalocheiritis, for example, in-herited nothing beyond the two embalmed figures of their father. The two eldest were given a half share each in Spiridion, while the youngest was forced by law to accept Theodora entire. He was obviously not content with this arrangement since he very soon relinquished the lady to the community. Spiridion, however, was a source of revenue as well as awe. By 1489 his two half shares were united in the possession of Philip the grandson—who made an attempt to carry off the relic to Venice, obviously to increase his turnover. This suggestion threw the island into a ferment, and he was forced to allow the tears and entreaties of the Corcyreans to prevail. Spiridion stayed but it was not till 1598 that he got his own church.

With the next generation the Saint became a dowry—for Philip's daughter Asimeni had little beyond her beauty, and marriages were as much forms of financial arrangement then as they are to-day.

The Saint was, so to speak, married into the Boulgaris family, and in their possession he has remained until to-day, universally loved and respected throughout the Ionian.

To the little figure in its casket the faithful bring posies of flowers and trinkets—but chiefly candles to back up their prayers. In the shady market-place outside the church there is a stall brimming with candles of all sizes, and here those who wish may buy anything from the smallest dip to a huge Chandler's Masterpiece, as long and thick as a man's arm. These candles give a strange impression, reminding one of stumps of human limbs smouldering in the dimness before the altar.

I must not forget to add that among the decorative motifs of the church is a wealth of Douanier-like paintings of shipwrecks, left as testimonials by thankful sailors whom the Saint helped into harbour in bad weather; there are also several pairs of unsolicited but accepted crutches. But the Saint is chiefly the patron of sailors, though his dominion can be extended in cases of need. Little children find him often in their dreams, a grim little figure of a man (not unlike General Montgomery) who knows exactly how to deal with croup, diphtheria, or lice.

Four times a year is the Saint's casket borne on a triumphal procession round the town; while on Christmas Eve and at Easter he is placed on a throne in the church and accessible to all comers. But the processions are something more than empty form. From early morning the streets are crowded with the gay scarves and head-chiefs of peasants from outlying districts who have come in to attend the service; every square is alive with hucksters' stalls sell-ing nuts, ginger-beer, ribbons, sweetmeats, carpet-strips, buttons, lemonade, penholders, bootlaces, toothpicks, lucky charms, ikons, wood carvings, candles, soap and religious objects. You will see the piled coiffures of Gastouri under their raving head-cloths of rose, yellow and blue; you will see the staid blue and white of the northern womenfolk, so like magpies; kilted Albanians in embroidered boleros, and woollen cross-gartered stockings—their womenfolk jingling in bracelets of coins; you will see the verminous Abbots of Fano and points north, and you will see the woollen-vested sailors of the opposite coast with their goathide belts and knives, and their moustache ends drawn back round their ears.

The sun shines brightly and the air sparkles with the Albanian snow-caps opposite; wild duck curve and scatter outside the gulf, and sails of madder, rose, bitumen, violet, are all trimmed in the direction of the old fort whose guns belch a salute in honour of the Saint.

The procession is led by the religious novices clad in blue cassocks and carrying gilt Venetian lanterns on long poles; they are followed by banners, heavy and tasselled, and rows of candles crowned with gold and trailing streamers. These huge pieces of wax are carried in a leather baldric—slung, as it were, at the hip. After them comes the town band—or rather the two municipal bands, bellowing and blasting, with brave brass helmets of a fire-brigade pattern, glittering with white plumes. Now troops in open order follow, backed by the first rows of priests in their stove pipe hats, each wearing a robe of unique colour and design—brocade of roses, maize, corn, grass-green, kingcup-yellow. It is like a flower bed moving.

At last the archbishop appears in all his pomp, and since he is the signal for the Saint to appear, all hands begin to make the sign of the cross and all lips to move in prayer.

The Saint is borne by six sailors under an old canopy of crimson and gold, supported by six silver poles and flanked by six priests. He is carried in a sort of sedan-chair, and through the screen his face appears to be more than ever remote, determined, and misanthropic. At the sight of him, however, warmth and happiness comes to every face. Radiantly happy the peasants turn from the procession to spend the long day dawdling over coffee or lemonade;

or bargaining over olives and livestock to take back with them on the island boats at nightfall. His brief appearance has qualified once more the terrors and ardours of living, and reminded them that he is there, still indefatigably on the job.

For the curious, St. Spiridion's Legendary will afford details of his adventures against the forces of heaven and earth—and his triumphs against them. For the contemporary sceptic there is a little booklet (sold for three drachmae at the steps of the church) in which one may read of more recent miracles. A policeman cured of epilepsy; the evil eye averted; an old man cured of the distressing gift of tongues.

Theodora Augusta, however, is now a barely distinguishable figure in the romance of Corfiot Saints; and to a large extent her powers have been taken over by a female saint—no less than St. Corcyra herself—with which modern hagiographers will have to deal. She is infinitely less interesting than Spiridion; and devotes most of her energies to causing dreams about buried treasure.

Spiridion is a formalist in his line; it is nearly always catastrophes to the community at large that he averts; yet he does not scorn the personal petition. Sit in the darkness of his church at midday and watch his petitioners; the deep shadow of the oak pews will hide you as you watch the reverence done and the waxen dip placed in the great brass quiver in which other candles are already burning.

Prayer is a form of bargaining; you will see at once that the psychological attitude to the Saint is one of rough familiarity. The tone of voice (that is to say the internal tone of voice—for the prayer is silent though the lips move) is the tone that one would adopt to a recalcitrant child. There is no question of humble pleading, and a foregone acceptance of refusal; the petitioner, whatever his request, assumes that it is most likely to be granted, and that it is consonant with the most elementary logic. It is what one could call 'a winning style', and it demands an equally resilient psychological attitude on the part of the Saint. Often such petitions are not only not granted—but other burdens as well are suddenly placed on the head of the unlucky petitioner. Thus Karamanos, the ugly boatbuilder of Nisaki, tried to obtain a cure for his epilepsy by prolonged prayer and the offering of numerous

The Island Saint

candles. Not only did his epilepsy get worse, but he contracted meningitis also and nearly died. His wife explained this by saying that the Saint had seen through him—and detected in him a loose-liver and foul-mouthed man. As he was the most moderate, faithful, just and hard-working character in the village one can only conclude that the Saint saw deeper than the rest of us—or else had confused him with his brother Basil who answered faithfully enough to this description.

At all events the Saint holds the island in his power; the boats that set out nightly for fishing or daily for foreign ports of call, all travel in his benign shadow; and it is he who welcomes you to port on the days when the deep-trenched north wind blanches the sea, and when the ironclads by the Venetian fort turn slowly on the leash to face it. It is he who guards your spirit when the wind screams down the ravines of Pantocrator. And when you are washed up in the dead calm of dawn, entangled like a sculpture in your broken boat and sprung nets—it is in his image and shadow that your soul finds rest. To him belongs the lovely greeting: Ὁ Ἅγιος Σπυρίδων μαζί σου.

III

Ionian Profiles

25.7.37

The sea's curious workmanship: bottle-green glass sucked smooth and porous by the waves: vitreous shells: wood stripped and cleaned, and bark swollen with salt: a bead: sea-charcoal, brittle and sticky: fronds of bladder-wart with their greasy marine skin and reptilian feel: rocks, gnawed and rubbed: sponges, heavy with tears: amber: bone: the sea.

Our life on this promontory has become like some flawless Euclidean statement. Night and sleep resolve and complete the day with their *quod erat demonstrandum*; and if, uneasily stirring before dawn, one stands for a moment to watch the morning star, which hangs like a drop of yellow dew in the east, it is not that sleep (which is like death in stories, beautiful) has been disrupted: it is the greater for this noiseless star, for the deep scented tree-line and the sea pensively washing and rewashing one dreams. So that, confused, you wonder at the overlapping of the edges of dream and reality, and turn to the breathing person in whose body, as in a sea-shell—echoes the systole and diastole of the waters.

Nights blue and geometric; endearing and seducing moon; the sky's curvature like an impress of an embrace while she rises—as if in one's own throat, so pure and glittering. When you have stared at her until she chills you, the human proportions of your world are reasserted suddenly. Suddenly the man crosses the orchard to the seawall. Helen walks with a lighted candle across the grass to tend the goat. Abstract from the balcony Bach begins to play—absorbed in his science of unknown relations, and only hurting us all because he implies experience he cannot state. And because paint and words are useless to fill the gap you lean forward and blow out the lamp, and sit listening, smelling the dense pure odour of the wick, and watching the silver rings play on the ceiling. And so to bed, two enviable subjects of the Wheel.

34

Ionian Profiles

Yesterday we awoke to find an Aegean brigantine anchored in the bay. She wore the name of *Saint Barbara* and two lovely big Aegean eyes painted on her prow with the legend Θεὸς ὁ Δίκαιος ('God the Just'). The reflected eyes started up at her from the lucent waters of the lagoon. Her crew ate melons and spoke barbarically—sounding like Cretans. But the whole Aegean was written in her lines, the great rounded poop, and her stylish rigging. She had strayed out of the world of dazzling white windmills and grey, uncultured rock; out of the bareness and dazzle of the blinding Aegean into our seventeenth-century Venetian richness. She had strayed from the world of Platonic forms into the world of Decoration.

Even her crew had a baked, dazed, sardonic look, and sought no contact with my chattering, friendly islanders. The brig put out at midday and headed northward to the Forty Saints in a crumple of red canvas. Like a weary dancer to the Forty Saints and the Albanian peaks, to mirror herself in some deserted and glassy bay like a mad butterfly. We could not bear to see her go.

My material is rapidly getting out of control once more. Theodore has been to stay for a few days. Characteristic of his shy heart he sends us presents. For N. a box of Turkish delight with pistachio-nuts in it; for me a flute made of brass, with the word Μοναξιά ('Loneliness') engraved upon it. It is impossible to get a note out of it so I have asked the peasants to find me the shepherd boy to teach me.

Theodore has recorded the latest miracle of St. Spiridion with sardonic humour. An old man from a country village appeared at the X-ray laboratory with what was diagnosed as an incurable cancer of the stomach; medicine having washed its hands of him, the old man and his family made a mass-petition to the Saint. Within three weeks he reappeared before the doctors. The cancer had been reabsorbed. Theodore is professionally downcast, but secretly elated to find that the Saint has lost none of his art. It gives him the opportunity for a long disquisition upon natural resistance. It appears that the peasants can stand almost any

35

physical injury which can be seen; but that a common cold may carry off a patient from sheer depression and terror. He gives an instance of a peasant who had a fight with his brother and whose head was literally cloven with an axe. Tying the two pieces of his skull together with a handkerchief the wounded man walked three miles into town to visit a doctor. He is still alive, though feeble-minded.

Zarian has contributed a wonderful piece of natural observation for our notebooks. He observed last Tuesday that the four clock-faces of the Saint's church all registered different times of day. Intrigued, he asked permission to examine the phenomenon, scenting an ecclesiastical mystery. But it turns out that the clock-hands are made of the flimsiest material and that the pressure of the wind upon the clock. . . . Therefore when the north wind blows the northern clock-face is slowed up considerably, while when the south wind takes up its tale the southern clock-face shows a loss of time.

Not that time itself is anything more than a word here. Peasant measurement of time and distance is done by cigarettes. Ask a peasant how far a village is and he will reply, nine times out of ten, that it is a matter of so many cigarettes.

30.7.37

It is important, when writing about the peasants, not to falsify them with sentimental humour. It is very much the fashion to represent them as comic and quaint abstractions attached to picturesque names like Paul and Socrates and Aristotle. The fact that they dress oddly seems to drive city-bred writers into a frenzy of romantic admiration. But really the average Balkan peasant is quite commonplace, as venal, cunning, or admirable, as a provinical townsman. And the sentiment which attaches to the pastoral life of these picturesque communities (which treasure amulets against the devil and believe in a patron saint), has been very much overdone. Anthropologists are only just beginning to visit the suburbs of our greater cities with their apparatus. Their findings should establish a greater sense of connection between the peasant and the townsman.

Ionian Profiles

Theodore has one particular friend who is a so-called lunatic. He sits with the others most of the time under the trees outside the whitewashed asylum building, looking at his own fingers; but at times an abrupt desire to talk seizes him, and when it does he unerringly selects for audience the so-called sane who pass along the dusty white road outside the railings. His name is Basil and he has yellow dilated eyes and a deep voice. Theodore often pauses on his way out of town to greet him, rattling his stick against the railings to draw his attention, and shifting the great green bag of tree-spore and seed which he carries about him on his walks. The lunatic sticks his head through the bars and smiles artfully. He says:

'They say I am mad.'

'Yes,' says Theodore gravely.

'And here I am.'

'Yes,' says Theodore.

'I am fed and clothed and do not have to work.'

'Yes.'

'Well—am I mad, or are the people outside mad?'

This is in the purest vein of Ionian logic and is to be commended to students of sociology. Basil's dossier lists him as a melancholic. A novice in a nearby monastery he early showed a gift for casuistry —that melancholy science. But he dips his fingers into Theodore's little paper bag of sweets with a transfiguring smile of happiness before he goes back to his place on the garden bench among the others.

'If you had an opportunity to put a question to Socrates what would it be?' writes Zarian. 'I would ask him if he was a happy man. I am sure that greater wisdom imposes a greater strain upon a man.' At the 'Partridge' this view is contested bitterly by Pel-tours and N. Wisdom, they say, teaches the ratiocinative faculty how to rest, to attain a deeper surrender of the whole self to the flux of time and space. Theodore recalls Socrates' epileptic fits while I find myself thinking of a line from Donne prefixed to 'Coryat's Crudities': 'When wilt thou be at full, Great Lunatique?'

Ionian Profiles

Fishing demands the philosophic attitude. We have been waiting a week for propitious nights to use the carbide lamp and the tridents and at last the wish has been granted: deep still water and a waning moon which will not rise until late.

After dinner I hear the low whistle of the man by the sea and I go out on to the balcony. He is shipping his basket and tridents and screwing his carbide-lamp to the prow. To-night I am to try my hand at this peculiar mode of fishing. The tridents are four in number and varying in size; besides them we ship the octopus hook—attached to a staff about the size of a billiard cue—for octopus is not stabbed direct but coaxed: whereas squid and fish are victims of a direct attack.

Small adjustments are made. He removes his coat which smells of glue and wood shavings and bales some of the water out from under the floor-boards. Then we cast off and move slowly out into the darkness. The night is deep and clean-smelling and utterly silent. Far out under the Albanian hills glow the little flares of other carbide-fishers. Anastasius circles in the margin of rocks below the house and begins to talk quietly, explaining his practice. Midges begin to fly into our faces and we draw down our sleeves to cover our arms. He rows standing up and turning his oars without breaking the surface—since it is into this spotless mirror that we must gaze, and the least motion of wind smears all vision.

Presently the carbide lamp is lit and the whole miraculous under-world of the lagoon bursts into a hollow bloom—it is like the soft beautiful incandescence of a gas-mantle lighting. Transformed, like figures in a miracle, we gaze down upon a sea-floor drifting with its canyons and forests and families in the faint undertow of the sea—like a just-breathing heart.

Now hoarse in the darkness beyond the point the Brindisi packet-boat brays once; and nearer a grampus gives a Blimp-like snort. Then we are alone again.

Anastasius talks quietly. When I am tired I must not hesitate to tell him, he says. He himself is indefatigable and in good weather fishes half the night. But he is not really talking to me; he is talking himself into the receptive watchfulness of the hunter—the un-reasoning abstraction which will allow him to anticipate the move-

Ionian Profiles

ment of fish; he is like a chess player combining possibilities in his own mind and testing them, so to speak, upon futurity.

We move in a concave ripple. Deep rock-surfaces, yellow and green and moving like a human scalp with marine fucus. Fishes, a school, the silver-white of σπάρος dawdle to the entrance of a cave and goggle at us. Each wears a black dapple on the back, and they look, in their surprise, like a row of semiquavers. Then, as if frightened by some purely marine event they disappear with the suddenness of a thrown switch. An eddy of wind purls the surface and Anastasius dips his twig of almond into the bottle of olive oil hanging at the prow. He scatters a few drops before us and the water clears again and steadies. I catch my breath, for there, crouching on a patch of reddish sand is the famous and eatable σκορπειὸς (I take him to be the sea-scorpion) with his bulldog head flattened upon a stone. Anastasius gets him squarely through the body at the first lunge and soon he is fluttering and ebbing in the darkness at my feet—a small dying pulse, uncomfortably tapping against the dry wood. Twice I put him in the basket and twice he leaps out and beats against the wood like the pulse of a dying bird.

We do not speak now, but proceed slowly along the edge of the lagoon in silence, surveying the haunted underworld which seems so like a panorama of the moon's surface. We stop where the fig-trees overhang and he tells me to look down. I can see nothing. Gingerly he lowers the trident and strikes; it is buried in a small white shape which begins to flutter madly. The small frightened eyes of the squid. As it breaks surface it spits a mouthful of ink over his face and arms and begins to wheeze like a sick kitten. Cursing softly and laughing he scrapes it off the trident against the gunwale and lets it drop into the basket where the contact of its fluttering hardly dead body suddenly rouses the stiffened body of the Scorpion to a small fluttering gasp of life. The air is cold to-night, and the sudden chill is fruitful, for within an hour we have several squid and two unnameable white fish besides the scorpion.

Anchored in a tiny bay we smoke a cigarette and Anastasius breaks off a piece of dry bread in his teeth. The air makes one hungry. The lamp is guttering and he charges it again with rock carbide. Once more the underworld flares into bloom. It is time, says Anastasius, for us to land an octopus, and to this end he ships the tridents and lets down his hooked staff, with its floating decoy of parsley training dispiritedly from it. He begins probing gently under rocks, turning this way and that. From the darkness of the cliff-edge above us a fir-cone falls with a little plop into the water. 'Look,' says Anastasius suddenly between his teeth, and I lean down. From under a rock, lazily moving, is something which looks like a snake. He is touching it very gently with the sprig of parsley, flirting with it. The tentacle plays softly with the leaves and is joined coyly by a second tentacle: then a third. They make playful passes at the sprig of green which conceals the waiting hook. Presently the ugly gas-mask head of the octopus comes into view, peering with moronic concentration at the decoy. And the moment has come. Anastasius slips the hook under the hood and tugs. There is a sudden strain and convulsion. The tentacles of the beast become rigid, but it is too late. Up it comes, writhing and grovelling, carrying two small boulders in its paws which it drops into the boat with a tremendous clatter, alarming us both. He now grips it firmly, and the hideous thing wraps itself round his arm, fighting back strongly. His object is to find the critical central bone, and he gives a sudden movement of the wrists, turning the hood inside out and plunging his teeth into a certain place in order to break it. A convulsion, and the whole mechanism seems to falter and fall to pieces. The tentacles still frantically suck and writhe, but they are now attached to a paralysed and shattered brain which gives them no directions for escape. Thrown dully to the bottom of the boat, they suck along the wood with the dull tearing noise that medical tape makes when it is being torn from human flesh.

Anastasius laughs softly and washes his hands in sea-water to dry them on the edge of his coat. A fish is a fish, but squid and octopus are a delicacy for him.

We take up the hunt in a desultory way and I manage, under his tuition, to spear yet another squid, and to miss a red mullet.

It is past midnight, and a small wind has sprung up, forcing us to use more and more olive oil to still the surface. We retrace our path slowly indulging in afterthoughts: looking under rocks which we have missed, and probing the larger caves in the hope of rousing an eel. Soon we are back at the davits, slinging the boat. Helen is there to meet us with bread and wine. I lend her my torch and she exclaims proudly over the catch in the happy vein of a person whose lunch and dinner for the morrow has been provided for.

By now a thin slice of moon is up, and early morning winds are beginning to curl up and lie on the surface of the water for a minute at a time before disappearing. The cypresses stretch for a moment from their romance stillness, like tired and cramped human models. I pause irresolute at the still edge of the bay, wondering whether the water is too cold for a bathe. The taste of the Greek cigarette is light and heady.

To-morrow I am to be instructed in the art of fishing with the shoulder net—called δείχτι. This has a span of about six feet, and is loaded at the edge with lead. It is carried folded in a certain way on the left shoulder and is used to trap fish in shallow water. The throwing of it demands a special skill.

And so, confused by these shallow veins of thought, to the balcony and the bedroom. The *Van Norden* lies at anchor twenty feet from the house, her tall spars rigid and consciously beautiful on the lacquer of the sea.

Sleep, in this cool, still room, is like entering a cave.

10.8.37

The Albanian smuggler has been over again from the Forty Saints. He is a fierce old ruffian, evil of manner and with no sense of humour. In his great sack he brought tobacco leaf, which we are buying for next to nothing. Anastasius teaches me how to strip each leaf of veins and lay them one on top of the other. Then we put them out to dry for a while, and finally to rest in the great magazine with its dry musty air and its rows of tomatoes drying on strings. Here after a while we roll and press the leaf and cut it finely with a razor blade. It is probably the coolest and richest pipe tobacco in the world, pure leaf and heavy. Anastasius loads his own cigarettes with it.

11.8.37

Took the *Van Norden* up in the direction of the Forty Saints in a strong western wind, but became totally becalmed in the lea of the headland, and lay off the Stephano lighthouse, watching a party refuel the lamp. It was strange to lie in this well of still water while not more than two hundred yards off the wind crisped the sea, and the air was wild with herring gulls. One of the lighthouse men tried to engage us in amiable conversation but at that range we could not understand a word he said, so we had to be content to wave to each other.

Zarian and his wife had arrived when we got back for tea, to stay a couple of days. Zarian says he has read somewhere that Nelson once drafted a plan to take the Old Fort (considered impregnable in his time) by running a frigate aground by the seawall, and boarding her from the masts. From every point of view a bad plan for there is a sea ramp which would have grounded the ship before her boarding crews were within reach of the lower battlements.

A letter from Zarian's wife in the south of the island.

'... You say I am your cruellest critic. I have been afraid when you seemed about to submit the island to the contamination of "fine writing"—but I need not have been. You will never touch it, my dear boy. Has the chapter upon Corcyra's perpetual spring been finished? I had it so much in mind that this walk southward with Theodore and the child has been like wandering through your book ahead of you. But how can you do it—how can anybody? There is as you say, no sense of season for the small ones. I have thrown away my paint box. Soon you will be throwing away your typewriter. All the summer children like iris and anemone, are out again—glades of them falling away to the White Cape, revived by the first autumn rains. Here it is your own underworld. My sketchbooks are fuller of notes than any Theodore could make it: speedwell, iris stylosa (?), marigolds, cranesbill, buttercup and pimpernel. Even the beady blue drops of grape hyacinth—how?

'You should do a sort of ballet of fruits and flowers; chorus the rough blue of sea, the staple olive-tone washed in rotation by the wild pearfoam, and the lands under Spartila by peachmist and asphodelcloud. It is too much. Mist of plum, pear, almond.

'Now we camped for the night in an orchard where nespoles in golden knots—but why go on? You must come and see for your-

self. Utterly silent and out of prehistory lay a little olive grove
shelving into the sea on a beach carpeted with brown dry seaweed.
We have been cooking from a friendly cottage with an earth floor,
the garden of it crammed with wistaria, carnation and stock—
drunk-making and rich.

'High up above me when I look up from this pad I see two
villages with cypresses on crags above us; where the ancient temple
was is now a small white-washed church—nothing has really
changed as you said. And the crags are alive with golden broom.
Kestrels hover and shriek over the blue gulf. A girl minds her
sheep and is friendly. Here it is the habit to keep a flower dangling
in the teeth—to set off the wonderful flashing smile.

'This morning when we went down for a bathe we found the
abbot of a local monastery sitting on a rock fishing for dear life.
He accepted a sandwich with great politeness and exchanged it
for a cigarette which he took from his stove-pipe hat, which meant
that he untidied his hair; he had to comb it out again and restore
the bun at the back.

'So you see how terribly unearthly we are becoming, just three
days in this haunted grove. And of course we have given your love
to everyone here.'

13.8.37

Father Nicholas is a great mythological character. He is a big-
boned rosy-faced old man of close on sixty-five. He likes to sit and
boast by the edge of the sea on calm days, like an Ionian Canute.
He is the author of three fine sons, one of whom is young Nicholas
the village schoolmaster. Under his pendulous trumpeter's cheeks,
under the sculptured fall of the great moustache, his mouth is
always smiling. He still wears the blue pantaloons, and curving
Turkish slippers of the older generation, and he is pedantic about
the whiteness of his three heavy silk shirts, two of which are always
out on the line being watched over by his timid, retiring wife.
Father Nicholas sits manfully in the shadow of his own vine, prod-
ding the grapes from time to time with his oak stick—in a faintly
sardonic manner, as if to dare them to ripen. He has the good-
humoured scolding manner—the scornful affection—which is the
mark of the finest Greek temperament. He boasts and boasts. The

story of his sailing voyages have become a sort of saga in his own mind; and when he begins a tale it is always to show how worthless the Ionians have become as sailors since the Diesel engine was imported. As he talks he consumes cup after cup of red wine, which is brought for him from a rapidly emptying keg in the magazine. His long nose ravens over the heavy Kastellani wine—his favourite brew. He illustrates his stories by drawing in the earth with his stick. The lack of variation in them is astonishing. In every one of them he is returning from Goumenitsa with a load of wood when he is overtaken by an immense 'fortuna'; everything goes overboard to lighten the craft; amidst thunder and lightning the ikon of Spiridion is consulted, but on this occasion the Saint is about other business because while they are praying a waterspout stoves in the boat. Father Nicholas at this point leaves the tiller and goes overboard clutching an armful of kindling (it is astonishing how few of these islanders can swim), which bears him up until he is washed ashore next day at Govino. All the crew perish, and the wife of Socrates, the mate, who is a woman of remarkable saintliness, is washed up two days later in Kouloura harbour. Her hands are folded on her breast and her eyes shut—Father Nicholas at this point folds his own hands, closes his eyes, and assumes an expression of saintly resignation. He is extremely affected by his own narrative, and wipes his eye in his sleeve, calling for more wine as he does so.

It goes without saying that Father Nicholas is an extremely cautious sailor; picking his wind, he occasionally makes an autumn trip over the water to Albania to gather a bit of fuel. But the slightest inequality of weather makes him run for harbour with a frantic and undignified haste. At home he is the complete autocrat, and spends all morning on the sunny terrace with a little plate of figs, bread, and olives before him.

He is occasionally guilty of an aphorism which sounds as if it were a proverb adapted by himself to suit his own experience. He enjoys uttering blood-curdling threats against his wife in the hearing of strangers, and she repays these with her quick sad smile and a remark which could only be translated as: 'Get along with you now.'

'Women', he grumbles, 'should be beaten like an olive-tree; but

44

in Corfu neither the women nor the olive-trees are beaten—because of the terrible laziness of everyone.'

We have given Nicholas a set of chessmen, and Theodore has managed to teach the game to the old man, who is delighted. Un-lettered as he is, he plays chess with tremendous imagination and certainty. When Theodore comes to stay he always strolls across to the little vine-wreathed balcony and challenges Father Nicholas to a game. More often than not he loses—and when this happens the old man becomes flushed with triumph, and begins to boast more than ever. 'What good are letters,' he rumbles affectionately, 'and learn-ing? Everything you have in your head, doctor, is little use against the wide-awakeness of the Romeos—the Greek.'

Theodore takes it meekly and in very good part. 'My learning tells, O Nicholas,' he replies, 'that if you continue to drink wine like this you will have an affection of the foot—which we have no name for in Greek. But it will be painful.'

'Bah,' says Father Nicholas equably. 'Since you cannot get the better of me in this game of bishops and kings, how can I believe you in other matters?'

In this flow of banter they disguise their affection for each other; for when Theodore is hunting for malaria specimens Father Nicholas will walk miles besides him to show him the location of a particular pond or well. While, whenever illness visits the family, either the sufferer or a letter is despatched at once by caique to Theodore in his laboratory. And we, as Theodore's friends, have become partly involved in these questions of the community's health. The encyclopaedia, a medicine chest, and a thermometer enable N. to perform miracles of diagnosis. So far we have success-fully diagnosed two cases of whooping cough, one malaria, one case of rheumatic fever, and a case of incipient rickets due to malnutrition.

15.11.37

You wake one morning in the late autumn and notice that the tone of everything has changed; the sky shines more deeply pearl, and the sun rises like a ball of blood—for the peaks of the Albanian hills are touched with snow. The sea has become leaden and slug-gish and the olives a deep platinum grey. Fires smoke in the villages, and the breath of Maria as she passes with her sheep to the headland, is faintly white upon the air. All morning she will sit crouched among the bracken and myrtle, singing in her small tired witch's voice, while the sheep-bells clonk dully around her. She is clad in a patchwork of rags, and leather slippers. In her hands she holds the spinning-bobbin upon which she is weaving her coarse woollen thread. Later on the treadle-loom in the magazine Helen will weave the coarse coloured blankets which the shepherd boys take into the hills with them where they mind their sheep in the deeper winter approaching. Maria watches the younger women picking olives through her wrinkled violet eyes and spits contemptuously before taking up her little song—which is about two ravens sitting in an olive-tree. Golden eagles hover in the grey. The cypresses hang above their own reflections like puffs of frozen grey smoke. Far out in the straits the black shape of a boat sits motionless—or dragging slowly and uncouthly with the flash of oars—like an insect upon a leaf. Now is the time to break logs for the great fireplace we have built ourselves, and smell the warm enriching odour of cypress wood, tar, varnish and linseed oil. It is time to prepare for the first gale of tears and sunsets from Albania and the East.

IV

Karaghiosis: The Laic Hero

We tie up at the old port on Tuesday and find little Ivan Zarian dancing down the great staircase under the lion of St. Mark to meet us. He has been waiting to tell us the great news. Karaghiosis has come to town and there is to be a performance this evening. All the children of the town and of course numbers of peasants will be there. We send Spiro to book seats for us all, and spend the afternoon sitting on the esplanade drinking lemonade in the white pure sunshine, and listening to clinking of ice in glasses around us. It is one of the innumerable Saints' days, and as such a whole holiday. The cafés are crowded, and the green grass of the Esplanade studded with the gay clothes of the Corfiot girls. Zarian, aroused from the abstraction into which his weekly Armenian literary article always throws him, discourses amiably about the art of the shadow-play. He has come across Karaghiosis under different guises in Turkey and in the Middle East, where the little black-eyed man wore, instead of his enormous prehensile baboon's arm, a phallus of equal dimensions. Translated into Greek he is no longer a symbol of pornographic buffoonery but something much more subtle—the embodiment of Greek character. It is a fertile theme. National character, says Zarian, is based upon the creations of the theatre. Huxley has remarked somewhere that Englishmen did not know how the Englishman should behave like until Falstaff was created; now the national character is so well established that everyone knows what to expect in the average Englishman. But what about the Greeks? Their national character is based on the idea of the impoverished and downtrodden little man getting the better of the world around him by sheer cunning. Add to this the salt of a self-deprecating humour and you have the immortal Greek. A man of impulse, full of boasts, impatient of slowness, quick of sympathy,

47

and inventive as well as assimilative. A coward and a hero at the same time; a man torn between his natural and heroic genius and his hopeless power of ratiocination.

In the middle of this discourse we are joined by Nimiec and Peltours who take an innocent delight in teasing Zarian; meanwhile the little Ivan is dancing about like a wasp waiting for it to get dark. As we have some shopping to do N. and I move off about our business with a promise to meet at 'The Partridge' for a glass of wine before we all go on to the shadow-play.

The shadows hang deep in the arcades by the little shop of Nomikos the bookbinder. He is binding some sketch-books for us. Farther down in what we call the Street of Smells, the ghosts of various dishes are being conjured up in great copper cauldrons: fish, sweetmeats, bread, onions.

The northerners are down for a dance; I catch a glimpse of Father Nicholas bending over a stall and haggling fearfully about the price of a cantaloupe. Farther on Sandos is walking in his Sunday clothes listening raptly to the cries and shouts of the hawkers, while his little black-eyed daughter walks beside him, sucking sweets. We have just time to do our shopping so that I dare not stop to talk. 'Will you come back with the caique to-night?' bawls Sandos, 'or did you come in the little '*lordiko*'[1] to-day?'

It is towards the hour of seven that, mellowed by the excellent wine of 'The Partridge', we cross the little cobbled square by the Church of the Saint, and seek our way through the alleys and fents of the Venetian town (the women touching hands as they talk on the balconies over our heads) to where the shadow-play is to be shown. In a little sunken garden by the Italian school the lights and the grumble of a crowd had already marked the place. A prodigious trade in ginger-beer and sweets is being carried on with the schoolchildren and the peasants who sit crammed into the small arena before the dazzling white screen upon which our hero is to appear. Two violins and a drum keep up a squalling sort of overture, punctuated by the giggles of the children and the pop

[1] The Van Norden is called 'the little lordcraft' by the peasants because of her upper-class lines.

of ginger beer bottles. (Important note. Ginger beer, first imported by the British during their occupation of the Ionian Islands has never lost its hold over the Corcyrean public. In places such as the Canoni tavern it may even be bought in those small stone bottles which we remember from our childhood, and which are quite as aesthetically beautiful as the ancient Greek lamp-bowls with which the museum is crammed.)

Our seats are right in front, where the orchestra can scrape away under our noses, and the sales of ginger beer increase noticeably owing to Ivan Zarian who persuades his father to buy us a bottle each. N. prefers nougat while Nimiec has found a paper-bag full of pea-nuts. Thus equipped we are prepared for the spectacle of Karaghiosis, whose Greek is sure to baffle us however much his antics amuse.

Presently the acetylene lamps on the hedge are extinguished, and the rows of eager faces are lit only by the light of the brilliant screen with its scarlet dado. The actors are taking up their dispositions, for now and then a shadow crosses the light, and the little peasant children cry out excitedly, hoping that it heralds the appearance of their hero. But the orchestra is still driving on with the awkward monotony of a squeaking shoe. I catch a glimpse of Father Nicholas at the end of a row, and seeing us smiling at him he feels called upon to make some little gesture which will put him, as it were, on the same plane as ourselves. He pushes aside the ginger-beer hawker, blows his nose loudly in a red handkerchief, and bawls to the tavern-keeper across the road in superior accents: 'Hey there, Niko—a submarine for my grandson if you please.' 'A submarine' is a charming fantasy; Nicholas' little grandson would much rather have a ginger beer but he is too experienced and tactful a child to interrupt the old boy. He sits vaguely smiling while the waiter darts across to them from the tavern with the 'submarine'—which consists of a spoonful of white mastic in a glass of water. Nothing more or less. The procedure is simple. You eat the mastic and drink the water to take the sweetness out of your mouth. While the child is doing this, and while Father Nicholas is looking around him, pleased at having caused a little extra trouble, and at having been original, the orchestra gives a final squeal and dies out. Now expectancy reaches its maxi-

Karaghiosis: the Laic Hero

mum intensity, for the familiar noise of sticks being rattled together sounds from behind the screen. This is a sign for the play to begin.

The crowd draws a sharp breath of familiarity and pleasure as the crapulous figure of Hadjiavatis lurches on to the screen, cocking an enormous eyebrow and muttering a few introductory remarks. 'It is Hadjiavatis,' cry the small children in the front row with piercing excitement, while Father Nicholas remarks audibly to the row behind him: 'It is the rogue Hadjiavatis.' But even his gruffness cannot disguise the affection in his tones, for Hadjiavatis is beloved for his utter imbecility. He is to Karaghiosis what Watson is to Sherlock Holmes—his butt and 'feed' at the same time. At the appearance of Hadjiavatis the orchestra strikes up a little jig—his signature tune—completely drowning his monologue, whereupon he gives an indignant shake of his whole body, commands it to be silent, and recommences his groans and exclamations. Apparently everything is rather gloomy. Nothing is right with him. He is poor, he cannot pay his rent, he has been recently set upon and badly beaten in mistake for someone else—in fact the whole universe is out of key. That is why he wanders erratically down this cardboard street with its fretwork houses searching for a friend—and of course there is only one friend that Hadjiavatis would go to seek in such a case. Karaghiosis. He bangs at the door of a hovel insistently and calls, 'Karaghiosis, are you there?' For a while there is no answer; the tension of the children is agony to watch. 'Are you there?' calls Hadjiavatis more insistently. A rather unsteady-looking coach passes across the stage almost running him over. He curses it, and recovering himself bangs ever more insistently at the door of the hovel. Finally a flap flies open and the head of the hero sticks out. At this a roar goes up from the children and a burst of joyous clapping which is hastily stilled in order not to miss what is being said. Karaghiosis has a great curved nose, a hump on his back, and the phallic arm already mentioned. He also has a wicked lidless eye, as ripe with mischief as a mulberry. 'You wish to speak to Karaghiosis?' he says with becoming caution. 'If it is about the rent then I am afraid Karaghiosis is not at home. As for the money you lent me last week I paid you back, as you no doubt remember.' With that he disappears and Hadjiavatis returns to his hammering once more. This time the head of one of Karaghiosis' innumerable children appears. Father is in bed and not to be disturbed. Hadjiavatis implores in nasal accents for an interview, but apparently Karaghiosis' wife refuses. Finally, in the course of the dialogue the word 'bread' is mentioned, and at this the front door flies open and the hero bounds out of it, asking in accents of hope and hunger: 'Did you say bread, O Hadjiavatis? Did I hear the word bread?'

Hadjiavatis manages to find a crust of bread on his person which he hands over to the famished Karaghiosis who agrees to talk to him at some length. Indeed their conversation lasts a considerable time, and is punctuated by the most endearing asides of the hero: 'A beautiful woman, did you say? Then keep her away from me. You know what it is. My beauty and charm—and, above all my social position—would make her fall in love with me immediately.'

Everyone is delighted by this kind of by-play. Karaghiosis' absurd vanity about himself is one of his strongest characteristics, and one which gets most of the laughs.

But the real problem which besets Hadjiavatis is one of power. Why should other people have carriages and servants and not he? Why indeed? echoes Karaghiosis, absently helping himself to some fruit off a fruit-stall.

'I tell you what,' says the hero at last. 'Would you like to be Prime Minister?' Hadjiavatis, despite his innumerable experiences of Karaghiosis' virtuosity in the matter of getting them both into trouble, eagerly agrees. 'Very well, then,' says Karaghiosis, 'have you any money?' It is apparently necessary to organize votes. Hadjiavatis unfortunately has only two drachmae which he is unwise enough to produce. The mulberry eye of the hero takes on a wicked glitter of cupidity and the children (who know quite well that whatever else happens, Hadjiavatis is sure to lose his money) roar with knowing laughter. Karaghiosis makes quite sure that the money is real and then, by one of those fertile and abrupt transitions for which his Hellenic mind is famous, he decides to make them both rich in a very short time. Hadjiavatis, like Doctor Watson, maintains a troubled faith in him while he shows a certain unwillingness to part with the money itself. 'It is simple,' says Karaghiosis, 'We will buy a bottle of wine for one drachma. We will sell it to the public at a drachma a glass. In that way we shall make considerable profit. With our profit we will buy more bottles of wine and sell them at a drachma a glass. In this way we shall become extremely rich and bribe enough voters to launch a party.' They traverse several celluloid squares, each garish in its many-coloured fretwork frame, and at last the bottle of wine is bought and they take up a station in the street to hawk their wares. Karaghiosis maintains a running fire of mild obscenities to attract the public—raw enough to keep the members of the audience in a roar. Old Father Nicholas is now laughing quite helplessly and unaffectedly, and wiping his eye in his sleeve, while his little grandson is laughing in little suppressed bursts, in order not to miss anything. Meanwhile on the stage things are not going too well. There is an altercation with a policeman; carriages pass; but few customers show any interest in the wine, and at last Karaghiosis says: 'Listen, Hadjiavatis. I have one drachma left over. Let me be the first customer. It is rather hot, and—who knows?—if we open the bottle it might stimulate trade. What do you say?' He pays over the drachma and Hadjiavatis carefully opens the wine and measures out a glass which the hero drinks with a rather over-done enjoyment. Meanwhile, Hadjiavatis himself is feeling the pangs of privation, and feels that he himself would like a glass of wine 'just to take the taste of dust out of his mouth'. The drachma changes hands again. Karaghiosis assures him that so long as the glass of wine is being paid for they need not fear for a profit, and this seems to console both of them—for very shortly Karaghiosis again feels rather faint and buys himself another glass, and Hadjiavatis again follows suit. This is agonizingly funny. Everyone is in a roar except one small spectacled child with a pale face, sitting in the front row, who leans forward and shouts: 'Hey, be careful, you are eating your capital.' A remark which is greeted with a further burst of laughter. The father of this budding bank manager (himself a clerk in a counting house) leans forward and pats the child's head approvingly.

And now of course the wine is finished, and the two puppets are busy trying to work out their profits. Karaghiosis' great mulberry eye cannot conceal his satisfaction while a certain thickening of his speech indicates that he is now full of a sense of warmth and well-being.

Karaghiosis: the Laic Hero

From now on the play becomes a surrealist fantasia. Their rise to fame is meteoric and is accomplished by the unblushing cunning of the hero, with Hadjiavatis suffering here and there for his errors of judgement. Almost nothing is too fantastic to present, and I can see from the glowing face of Father Nicholas that what our surrealist friends might call 'the triumph over causality' is considerably older than Breton—and indeed is an integral part of all peasant art. The succession of figures on the dazzling screen glow with a kind of brittle life of their own; the voices (whose volume and pitch betray their human origin) crackle and spark with a kind of suppressed hysteria. All Greece is in this scene; the market-place, the row of Turkish figures, the wonderful power and elasticity of thought and verbal felicity; the tenderness and vulgarity of Karaghiosis; and all indicated with so little of the landscape to which I had hoped to be a guide. Karaghiosis, whose humour is cast in a townsman's mould, is still surrounded by memories of the day when he and his kind were mad, violent clansmen in the hills around Olympus: or scattered colonies across the Black Sea, still tenaciously holding to an optative mood and a pronunciation which Piraeus has forgotten or only remembers as a joke. On this little dazzling screen you have the whole laic mystery of Greece which has been so long dormant in the mountains and islands—in the groves and valleys of the archipelago. You have the spirit and the unconquerable adaptability of the Greek who has penetrated with the leaven of his mercuric irony and humour into every quarter of the globe.

By now we have met a number of characters who are to become familiar in the immortal Karaghiosis cycle of plays. There is Gnio-Gnio, a lunatic figure in a top hat and cutaway coat, whose singing Zante accent is a joy to listen to. There are the Salonika Jews, each tiny and clad in a shapeless sack-like robe, out of which they speak shrill and clever, hands firmly folded in front of them. There is even an unusual figure called 'The Lord' who is dressed in what Father Nicholas must imagine to be the conventional English fashion—in a tail-coat, buttonhole, spats, and a topper. There is also the appalling Stavrakas of Piraeus whose vanity and vulgarity make him justly the object of little children's derision. There is the Grand Vizier, a most sympathetic figure, and of imposing size—not to mention the Cadi, who orders beatings with a cool impersonal air of detachment.

The drama reaches its peak with a faked election, in which Karaghiosis, in order to win, manages to resurrect all the corpses in the local cemeteries, who pass in a grisly single-file across the stage to the polling booth to vote for the hero.

And now, with abrupt suddenness Karaghiosis appears to recite a short epilogue and while the applause is still deafening us, the screen goes out and we are in darkness. The orchestra has long since packed up, and we stumble yawning from the garden in the darkness, pressed all about by the eager bodies of the children. The warm sign of 'The Partridge' welcomes us and the company is enriched to-night by the seldom presence of Nimiec, who has tales to tell about the caves off the north end of the Saint Angelo cape. He has just spent a week with the fishermen there trying to catch a shark. Zarian is in form too. His memory has been strengthened and awakened by Karaghiosis, and he has stories about Georgia and the Caucasus dancers which will last well into the night. Only Theodore, whose constancy in erudition is the marvel and envy of all of us, has succumbed to the lure of documentation and is writing a few notes on the back of the menu, which must be incorporated in the book. There is some fresh squid, smoking hot with green vegetables, and some Spartila wine to whet the appetites of our imaginations; and to round it all off, the three puppet-players drop in to the tavern for a glass of wine. The leader is a sharp-featured young man, whose sallow boredom of expression conceals his gifts of mimicry and satire; his helpers are both small and podgy and nondescript of feature. All three are clad in cheap suits and felt hats. Invited to a glass of wine they sit awkwardly among so many 'foreigners' and answer questions with pleasure; I think they distrust our interest in the shadow-play; there is the faint Greek suspicion at the back of their minds that they are the victims of a misplaced politeness; also why the bearded professorial gentleman should be writing details about Karaghiosis on the back of a menu is rather a mystery. But Theodore's charming mildness and the convivial bacchic warmth of Zarian soon thaws their shyness. Also the blind fiddler's son has begun his acrid tunes on the violin, standing by the chair of his

Karaghiosis: the Laic Hero

father—and under cover of the music and the clink of glasses confidences are easier. They come from Patras. Every year in the autumn they play up as far as Preveza, and then come across the straits to tour Corcyra, Cephalonia and Zante. One of them has a couple of the Karaghiosis chap-books in his pocket, and, turning from the garish cover (which shows the hero engaged in ferocious argument with the Vizier) I happen upon a list of some hundred titles of plays which deal with the adventures of this latest addition to the Greek Pantheon. 'Karaghiosis the Architect', 'Karaghiosis the Martyr of Virtue', 'Karaghiosis the Archaeologist', 'Karaghiosis in Love', 'Karaghiosis the Financier'.

Meanwhile Theodore has compiled his list of characters with the help of the saturnine young man, while Zarian is well and truly launched upon an anecdote about his early life in Armenia, his mane of silver hair flying and his expressive voice rolling. The copper cauldrons are smoking, while the scavenging cats are feasting piteously all round our feet, and the wooden sign of the 'Partridge' is swinging in a light breeze—a good augury for the night journey home. Calm, upon the dark calmness of the night outside, the tangoid music of the guitar and the fiddle grazes and moves; banal but wonderfully moving, the words are taken up by the diners, until even the cook beats with a ladle on a cooking-pot to mark the time.

The three players take their leave with warmth, promising us to play us any piece of our choice the following day, and Zarian shakes hands warmly with each while continuing his faultless recitation of adventures in French to Nimiec, whose energies are divided between laughing and feeding a tabby cat under the table.

It is after midnight when we separate, N. guarding the precious menu upon which the fruits of Theodore's scholarship are written in his flawless miniscule handwriting. The port is dark, and alive with the lick and slap of dark water; there is a spark of light off Stiletto; wind south-westerly upon a clean tranquil darkness. The little boat rides clear in her white awnings; turns to Albania her sharp cheeks, and slides clear of the fort. And so home to the white house, tired and happy, and with a sense of many blessings.

'Karaghiosis,' writes Theodore, 'and the shadow-play which created him, are both ancient. The tradition of the hero in drama

Karaghiosis: the Laic Hero

is medieval. His adventures rival those of Tyll Owlglasse in the German—and his place in the popular imagination is one which one could compare with the Elizabethan Tarleton. The disturber of social justice, he never does anything to alienate the audience, and his political licence is almost absolute (for example, despite the Metaxas dictatorship Karaghiosis enjoyed uninterrupted powers of critical comment, at a time when even Plato was banned in the University of Athens—or at least expurgated). He is the spirit of the little man—but the Greek little man; he is splendid at loafing, borrowing, and playing practical jokes on his friends which have a strong profit-motive. He is a current symbol for the whole Middle East under varying forms. The comic phallus, we have already noticed, has been translated into an arm so long and so expressive as almost to satisfy the psychological theory of symbolic substitution. The fun is not by any means clean fun by puritan standards and nothing like it would be allowed on the stage in London; but is essentially pure in that it is broad and unmalicious. The list of characters which appear from time to time in the Karaghiosis mythology is quite considerable; of his own family there is first of all his wife (Karaghiozaina: *Καραγχιόζαινα*). She is quite conventional, while his numberless children (Kollitiri: *Κολλιτίρι*) supply unvarying comic relief without becoming distinguishable from the average street urchin. Karaghiosis' uncle (Barba Giorgos: *Μπάρμπα Γιῶργος*) is made of sterner stuff. A shepherd from the mountains, he wears the fabulous foustanella and speaks with the crackling dialect of Aitolia and Akarnania. His huge moustaches bristle with avarice and friendliness. Gullible at times he is usually honest and bold. His particular opposite number is Dervenagas (*Δερβέναγας*) who is Albanian and resembles Barba Giorgos in many ways. Their meetings are usually accompanied by tremendous tussles in which Dervenagas is almost always beaten. Karaghiosis dislikes him hotly and takes every opportunity of humiliating him. The Vizier, the Aga, and the Cadi are conventionalized Turkish figures of extraordinary size; the former is the most important and is on the whole sympathetically represented.

Hadjiavatis is the Turkish town crier and is associated with all Karaghiosis' rascalities—in which he usually suffers instead of their author. Next in importance come Sir Gnio-Gnio and Captain Nikolis. Gnio Gnio (*Νιόνιο*) is an idiotic, lisping imbecile in a top hat and tail-coat with a long pointed beard. He represents Zante, and speaks with the curdling sing-song accents of the island. This of course is from our point of view. It is presumed that when in Zante he represents Corcyra with a changed but still sing-song voice. Captain Nikolis is a makeweight (*Καπετὰν Νικολης*) whose atmospheric value lies in his baggy breeches and his Aegean fez.

And now we move from character to myth; for Alexander the Great (*ὁ Μέγας 'Αλέξανδρος*) survives still in the Karaghiosis cycle of plays as a huge warrior dressed in full armour. He even kills the dragon (*τό θεριὸ*) in certain plays, and obviously owes something to St. George. Next comes Morphonios (*Μορφωνιός*) though exactly what he is one cannot decide. A hideous mommet with a vast lolling cranium, he speaks with a frantic affectation of voice, and dresses in conventional European clothes. He is sometimes played off against Stavrakas (*Στάβρακας*) an extremely nasty specimen of Piraeus bravo clad in exaggerated modern dress and felt hat—which, in the course of his lengthy conversations, he is in the habit of cocking over one eye. His self-assurance is the comic vein in him, and this Karaghiosis exploits to the full.

To bring up the tail-end of this procession one could list The Lord or The Frank (*ὁ Λόρδος, ὁ Φράγγος*) tail-coated representatives of European culture, as well as Abraham, Moses, Isaac, etc., an endless series of Salonika Jews, uniform in size, dress and accent. Female figures seem very unimportant in the plays, and besides Karaghiosis' wife they include an occasional Vizier's daughter, a princess, and a wife of Barba Giorgos.

The puppets themselves are the result of curious workmanship; since their dimensions of operation are so limited, and since the light which illuminates them comes from behind the screen, it is necessary to do as much filigree-work as possible to enliven the bare outlines of the figures. Great ingenuity is shown in their manufacture, and the use of a kind of many-coloured gelatine material enables their clothes to be as brightly coloured as those of the island peasants themselves.

Karaghiosis: the Laic Hero

18.10.37

Three days of squall and rain. The wind moans on the promontory, and all day long the threshing of sea sounds on the white
rock outside the house. In the interval as the undertow draws back
you hear the dull patient throb of the hand-loom in the magazine,
and the cough of the old billy-goat. Trees lean and whirl where the
wind pours through the vents and boulder-strewn crevices of Pantocrator. The roof has been sprung in several places, but this is the
first taste of winter, and it is good that we should be proven wind-
and-water-tight before the real thunderstorms of December.
Theodore has unearthed another charm against accident; it is for
fair-weather sailors on moonlit nights. 'It is widely believed that
the figure of a woman rising from the sea beside the boat calls out
in wild accents "How is it with Alexander?" (*Τί κάνει ὁ Μέγας
'Αλέξανδρος*). The correct answer for those who do not want their
craft overturned by her rage and grief is "He lives and reigns still"
(*Ζεῖ καί βασιλεύει*). I do not know whether this charm will be of
any practical assistance to you, but since you say you always
run out to the Bay of Fauns at the full moon, it would be better
on the whole to memorize it. One can never tell.'

I ask Anastasius about the belief. He denies it with rather an
uncomfortable look. He likes to consider himself superior in intelli-
gence to the ordinary peasants, but I can tell from his manner that
he has heard of it. 'Does old Nicholas believe it?' I ask, and he turns
his black eyes out of the window for a full minute before shrugging
his shoulders and replying 'How can I tell what these old men
believe? He cannot read and write.' Father Nicholas is not an heir
to our common European culture!

V

History and Conjecture

12.9.37

Confused by our clumsy gestures of interpretation, history is never kind to those who expect anything of her. Under the formal pageant of events which we have dignified by our interest, the land changes very little, and the structure of the basic self of man hardly at all. In this landscape observed objects still retain a kind of mythological form—so that though chronologically we are separated from Ulysses by hundreds of years in time, yet we dwell in his shadow. Like earnest mastodons petrified in the forests of their own apparatus the archeologists come and go, each with his pocket Odyssey and his lack of modern Greek. Diligently working upon the refuse-heaps of some township for a number of years they erect on the basis of a few sherds or a piece of dramatic drainage, a sickly and enfeebled portrait of a way of life. How true it is we cannot say; but if an Eskimo were asked to describe our way of life, deducing all his evidence from a search in a contemporary refuse dump, his picture might lack certain formidable essentials. Thus Ulysses can only be ratified as an historical figure with the help of the fishermen who to-day sit in the smoky tavern of 'The Dragon' playing cards and waiting for the wind to change. The Odyssey is a bore, badly constructed and shapeless, dignified by poetry everywhere degenerating into self-pity and rhetoric; the characters are stylized to the point of irritation, and their conventionalized drama serves simply as a decorative frame for the descriptive gift of the author which is a formidable piece of equipment.

Yet with what delightful and poignant accuracy does the poem describe the modern Greeks; it is a portrait of a nation which rings as clear to-day as when it was written. The loquacity, the shy cunning, the mendacity, the generosity, the cowardice and bravery, the almost comical inability of self-analysis. The unloving humour and the scolding. Nowhere is it possible to find a flaw.

History and Conjecture

Three towns contend for Ulysses and Nausicaa; Kassopi in the north, with its gigantic plane-tree and good harbour, its bluff ilex-grown fortress where the goats graze all day, might have well been a site for such a fantasy. Fronting the ragged scarps of Albania, the north wind fetches in the blue sea with a crisp lazy power quite foreign to the gulf. South of Corfu town, the peninsula of Paleopolis is supposed to be the site of the ancient town; but there is nothing left of the arcades and the fountains and columns of the fabulous capital. The shadow of the marshy lake is hardly disturbed by the ripple of water from Cressida's stream. Dried out Venetian salt-pans have eaten away the original form of the lake and here the sea settles in tideless green stagnation, a haunt for pelicans, wild duck and snipe. In the dazzle of the bay stands Mouse Island whose romance of line and form (white monastery, monks, cypresses) defies paint and lens, as well as the feebler word. This petrified rock is the boat, they say, turned to stone as a punishment for taking Ulysses home. It might have been here.

Last and most likely is Paleocastrizza, drenched in the silver of olives on the north-western coast. The little bay lies in a trance, drugged with its own extraordinary perfection—a conspiracy of light, air, blue sea, and cypresses. The rock faces splinter the light and reflect it both upward and downward: so that, staring through the broken dazzle of the Ionian sun, the quiet bather in his boat can at the same time look down into three fathoms of water with neither rock nor weed to interrupt the play of the imagination: so that, diving, he may imagine himself breaching the very floor of space itself, until his fingers touch the heavy lush sand: so that, rising to the surface borne upward by air and muscle he feels that it is not only the blue sky that he breaks open with his arms, but the very ceiling of heaven. Here are the grottoes. Paleocatrizza has two of them, one reachable by boat and beautiful. The walls are twisted painfully out of volcanic muscle, blood-red, purple, green, and nacreous. A place for resolutions and the meetings of those whose love is timid and undeclared.

For the benefit of the more recondite, or for the mere specialist, one must record the existence of a great cave in the point immediately before the beach marked Hermones on the maps. It is

approachable only when there is a calm, and the entrance is imposing, being formed in the style of a great gateway. Empty
plaques of metamorphic stone stand above, as if the inscriptions
have been melted from them. The entrance is knee-deep in water
and slimy with rock; but this first cave leads to a second, higher and
drier. The walls of this are palpitant with the bodies of bats, which
hang like a heavy curtain, trembling and squeaking at any intruding noise. This second cave is perhaps ten yards across and as high
—and in one corner, like the secret to one of those puzzles one has
sought for a lifetime, opens a door. There is space enough to pass
if one stoops. Nothing is revealed beyond this barrier. For those
who have the courage and the curiosity to proceed, a torch is
necessary.

At first nothing; a rubbish-heap of broken stones at the beginning of a corridor. But a clearly defined corridor leading, it seems,
into the very heart of the earth. Within twenty paces it branches
into a multiplicity of corridors—like a dream, or a poem too
charged with allusions—and the walls become heavy and damp,
as if with mist. It seems a thousand miles away that the summer,
with its quickened heart-beat of cicadas and wind, livens the
meadows of Corcyra; we are here, deep in the ground, and our
voices are low as if they sensed the dreadful unyielding rock which
surrounds us. The many corridors menace us.

'We will never remember the way back,' says N.

The torchlight is barren and futile with its white beam moving
along the walls. Holding N.'s hand I am aware of the small resist-
ing pulse of the heart-beat like a message to say that we are not
really part of it—the echoing and uncomfortable night of the rocks.

In 1912 a scientist tried to negotiate the corridor, using a light
twine as a guide; but somewhere in the heart of the world the
twine broke, and, it is presumed, his torch gave out, for he never
reappeared in the light of day. This story, which I invent to
frighten N., brings back to us both the seducing sweetness of life
there outside the cave; the fishermen at their lobster-pots, and the
whole endearment of the Valley of Ropa, with its dapple of vines
and figs. The soft throaty call of turtles in the arbours above
Perama. The poison-green line of water perching and falling upon
the shoals off the northern point.

History and Conjecture

The walls of the outer cave tremble in their membrane-like covering of bats; strange shudderings and copulations, strange disturbances and awakenings, strange departures and arrivals—like the unconscious in its outlawed slumber. One's own flesh has become chill and puckered by the cold of the place. Very dimly now the sea can be heard outside, familiar as snoring, rapping and licking its way among the rocks. The pools are empty of fish.

The little white boat rides glib and pert in the shadow of the cliff, with Niko anxious at the tiller; wind has sprung up from the south-west, and the breakers are beginning their clock-like momentum sheer from the shores of Africa. It is time to make the half-hour run for the narrow harbour of Paleocastrizza. Shaken free, the sails immediately draw like a white fire, and crisp at the lips of the *Van Norden*, the sea draws her seething line of white. In the spaces of the wind the ear picks up the dry morse-like communication of the cicadas high above on the cliffs; while higher still in space sounds the sour brassy note of a woman's voice singing. N. caught in one of those fine unconscious attitudes sits at the prow, head thrown back, lips parted, long fair hair blown back over the ears—the doe's pointed ears. Drinking the wind like some imagined figurehead on a prehistoric prow one cannot tell from the sad expression of the clear face whether she hears the singing or not. Or whether indeed the singing is not in one's own mind, riding clear and high above the white sails to where the eagles, broken like morsels of rock, fall and recover and fall again down the invisible stairways of the blue. How little of this can ever be caught in words. The last clear point comes out to meet us with the little rock-chapel and lighthouse standing clear. The *Van Norden* turns, trembles for an instant between opposing intentions, and then dives clear through the towering walls of rock, into the bay where Nausicaa found the timorous Hero, washed up as naked as Adam but twice as intelligent.

20.9.37

It is one of the peculiar sentimentalities of the historian, this perpetual desire to trace places and origins by the shallow facts of romance. Fano, a few hours north of Paleocastrizza, is supposed to be Calypso's island—'the sea-girt isle set with trees'. Corcyra, then, is the home of the oar-loving Phaeacians, and the place of Ulysses' meeting with Nausicaa. It is of course the final unkindness that the few scanty facts in Homer's record of the adventure do not offer the historian any help. For Ulysses on his raft, helped by a fair wind, took eighteen days to cover the few sea-miles separating Fano and Corcyra. At least if one is to be browbeaten by such absurdities. Zarian has effectively disposed of this kind of thing in his essay on *Cowardice Among Historians*, from which Theodore has translated the following passage: 'We refuse to be confounded by facts like these. Firstly it is necessary to this enchanted island that its landscape should be sweetened by such a fantasy, and secondly the Ancient Greeks had no sense either of time or distance. No reliance can be placed on their measurements, just as no reliance can be placed on the modern Greeks when they are dealing with space and time. Among the peasants to-day the duration of a cigarette is used to record distance in space. A peasant, asked how far a village is will reply: 'Two cigarettes.' If you reply that you do not smoke he will, with difficulty, hunt about in his mind for the words 'hours' or 'minutes', but it will be quite obvious from his use of them that he has only a very faint conception of what they mean. I maintain that the same holds true of the Ancient Greeks. Deft at the delineation of a psychology which has remained constant until to-day, Homer was all at sea when it came to accurate fact. Thus we are prepared to convict Homer of normal Greek mendacity rather than admit the suggestion that Ulysses did *not* land in this wave-washed cove, his skin bleached and worn like an old sea-shell from the exposure to the elements.'

To the lovers of Paleocastrizza this passage will make a certain appeal; but perhaps this emphasis on Greek character will seem a little wearisome to those whose only interest in Greece begins and ends among the broken columns of prehistory. After all, one might say, what contact could exist between the refined and isolated life of Ancient Greece, and the haphazard life of the modern Greek living in the shadow of Europe, under the inferiority-complex of the top hat? One incident will provide an answer.

Anastasius knows that I am collecting peasant stories; the lunch hour of the workman is the time for smoking, lounging and story-telling, and from time to time when his work brings him into contact with the masons and plasterers of Vigla up the hill, he occasionally comes home with a story about St. Corcyra, or the tale of a haunted well.

Last week we were aware, during the evening, of an unusual disturbance in the family next door. Instead of retiring early to bed, the little oil lamp was burning until after midnight. We heard voices—the voice of Sky in particular—talking and laughing. There was a note of excitement; and the drone of Helen's voice reading aloud. It was unusual for them to stay up late and waste lamp oil, and it was particularly unusual for the children to be awake late.

Next morning Anastasius, still unshaven, appeared at the breakfast table and said with some enthusiasm that he wished my Greek were good enough for him to relate me an 'extraordinary' story; but it was rather complicated in its details. It was about a man called Odysseus who was washed up on an island. As he spoke I noticed that he was holding a small book crumpled in his hand. He handed it to me. It was a first-form primer as used by the village school; it was an account of the Odyssey written in very simple demotic Greek for schools. Little Sky, he explained, had gone to school for the first time the day before, and had returned home at night with this book. In helping her read the first chapter he had suddenly found himself reading the story of Ulysses for the first time. To be sure, he had heard of Homer, but even now there seemed to be little connection in his mind between this delightful tale which had kept the whole family up until after midnight, and the revered name. 'It is such a pity,' he kept repeating, 'that you will not understand it. It is one of the best things I have ever heard —this fable (παραμῦθι).'

When I told him as well as I could that I had already heard the story he was extremely doubtful.

'But the books,' he said, 'are printed in Athens.'

'Yes, but the story is very old. In schools in England the children are made to read it.'

'About Odysseus?'

'Himself.'

'And Penelope?'

'All the same people.'

History and Conjecture

He looked so doubtful and unconvinced that I took him into the drawing-room and found the big English translation of the Odyssey with the ancient Greek medallions on the cover. He spelt out the name of Homer and shook his head uneasily.

'I don't understand,' he said uneasily. 'Then is the story true?'

'Quite true,' I said. 'When Odysseus reached here from Fano —'

'What is that?' he said eagerly. 'What is that?'

'Don't you know that it was here that Nausicaa lived, that the palace of the King was in Corcyra?'

'Before God?'

'Before God. You know Paleocastrizza?'

'Yes.'

'You know the first of the three bays, before the hotel?'

'Yes.'

'There they met. Odysseus arrived there from Fano where at that time Calypso lived.'

His concern and pleasure were delightful to watch. He stood uncertainly in the doorway holding the primer in his hand, not knowing what to say. 'I do not understand,' he said once more. 'It is very strange.'

Later I saw him walk down the cobbled path to where old Father Nicholas sat on a chair, his blue trousered legs set apart manfully. His stick lay across his right knee. On his left knee he was balancing a plate of bread and onions. I saw Anastasius showing him the little book and repeating what I had told him. Two days later he asked me on the next trip round the island to take him and Sky, because he wanted to see the place where Odysseus had been washed up.

25.9.37

Kassopi, among the other candidates, has a style entirely its own. In spring, meadows back it, starred with the foam of wild flowers. The village finds its axis in a giant tree whose shadow falls equally upon the tavern and the church. A good harbour, Kassopi is the port of call for the carbide fishers, and under the ancient fortress the waves shatter themselves upon ledges of clean granite and arcs of dazzling pebbles. Empty beaches to the north and south stun

65

you by their silence and emptiness, and the egg-like perfection of the pebbles. Here and there, in patches of sand, you may see the weird ideograms left by the feet of herring-gulls, the only visitors. Visitors from Rome came here in the past for summers of indolence and solitude. Tiberius, it is said, had a summer villa here, now swallowed by the sea; and here the mad flabby Nero (who had translated himself from a weak human being into a symbol of kingship and all its evils) sang and danced horribly at the ancient altar to Zeus. Tibullus, Cato and the tedious Cicero passed down this channel on the way to Dyrrachium.

Kassopi must be seen on a festival day, when the great circle of coloured women tread hypnotically in a circle under the branches of the plane-tree, and mingled with the sharp whimpering of the bagpipes and fiddles, the flat stabs of the drum, you can hear the excited shouts of the crowd, and the mad giggling of the donkeys. A row of gay caiques drawn up at the beach; the tavern over-flowing with all manner of visitors; sellers of cakes and ribbons and trifles; the priests sitting gravely in the shadow of the porch drinking a glass of wine. The magpie mountain women, glad to relax after their eternity of olive-gathering. The moustached Albanians with their bandoliers; the blue Dalmatian policemen with their musical comedy frown; and a great pure wind beating the waves of the bay into chaff.

The ramparts of the fortress are deserted. Here, it is said, the inhabitants of the town can hear the chink of armour and the foot-falls of ghostly Roman sentries changing guard; and it was in the little harbour below that we discovered the remains (for so we thought them to be) of Tiberius' summer villa, or else of the for-gotten temple of Zeus. One summer evening we tied up in the harbour and, it then being tea-time, went over the side for a swim, while Niko brought out the food. We had just received a pair of diver's goggles, which transform the under-water world into a miracle of clarity. Idly playing, in about two fathoms, I saw a Greek newspaper lying on the lucent floor of the bay, moved slowly by the current, and decided to see whether I could make out the headlines in the green gloom below. Three feet from the floor I struck an icy vein of water which pushed me back with some force. It was so cold that involuntarily I opened my mouth and drew in a mouthful. It was fresh water. At the same moment the current moved the thick green fronds of seaweed aside and I saw the irregular coping of a well-top, and the faint white marks which seemed to me to look like an overgrown garden path. This was so exciting, and the stone-work so obviously man-made, that N. and L. and myself spent half an hour trying to clear the seaweed which obstructed the view, or to move one of the stones. But such an attempt would need tackle, good divers, and a calm day to be successful. Yet the sweet spring plays there, in the middle of the harbour; in the sunken garden of Tiberius' summer villa. No one seemed to have noticed it; neither the priest, nor the policeman nor the barber. Nor did they show any interest. Kassopi was too busy with her great dance to bother with trifles.

28.9.37

I must not forget to mention that Kassopi does not boast a petrified rock in the shape of a boat; Mouse Island suggests to the lovers of Paleopolis that it was here that the weary rowers on their return from Ithaca were swallowed up in the stony wrath of Poseidon. While off Paleocastrizza there is another and more perfect rock which resembles the fantastic boat much more closely. Zarian never fails to take his friends up the steep road to Lakones to gaze out across the dazzle of waters towards this motionless boat. It is sufficient corroboration for him.

29.9.37

Across the rich screen of this landscape many names, ancient and modern, offer themselves to the mind like the translation of flesh into ghostly appearances which still delude the living by their resemblance to them.

Corcyra's history is a chequer-board; little of it is interesting because of its variety of detail, and the stubborn sameness of the general pattern. Spawned by Corinth, she was sensible enough to assert herself as a maritime force during the Persian War of 475. Herodotus' scornful account of her treachery has earned him the withering vituperation of Zarian in more than one Armenian article. Xenophon, writing of the Spartan invasion under Mnesippus, records a paradise of fertility and cultivation; a paradise so rich in loot that it unmanned the invaders and glutted them with booty in food and oxen, fruit, sculpture and slant-eyed Corcyrean girls.

In this noble harbour Augustus gathered together his fleet for a battle which gave him a world.

Guiscard conquered her, one of the twelve sons of Tancred, and in aspect as terrible and bold as any Teutonic God. Gibbon's podgy prose commends for 'patient vigour of health and commanding dignity of form' while we are informed that the Apulian poet praised him for excelling the cunning of Ulysses and the eloquence of Cicero. Invested Duke of Calabria, he crossed to Sicily in an open boat, and won the island by incredible endurance in hardship. The saga of his life and adventures still awaits a chronicler apt enough for so great a theme.

Richard the Lion paused here on his way back from the farcical adventure of Cyprus.

Michael the Despot reigned and fell.

Caught for an instant assembled in the great harbour, Villehardouin spent some magical words on the shabby hirelings of the fourth Crusade: 'The wind was favourable, and the sky pure and serene, and a profound calm reigned over the waters. Three hundred vessels of all sizes with their colours afloat from their sterns, covered a vast space. The helmets and cuirasses of the 30,000 warriors reflected back the rays of the sun. And now over the waters came the hymns of priests, invoking heavenly blessings, and the tones of the soldiers, lightening the leisure of the voyage with martial songs, the winding of horns and the neighing of horses all mingled with the splashing of oars.' Impenitent glory of that Whitsun Eve, with the great fleet motionless on the shining mirror of the bay. 'I bear you witness,' he cries, 'that never was so gallant a sight seen.'

And then the sleek Genoese Vetrano, fattened with politics and cruelty, described impartially as pirate or admiral. He is Zarian's favourite character. Never, says Zarian, were the Venetians more at fault than when they did him to death.

Corcyra, like her St. Spiridion, was once a dowry for a beautiful woman, destined for a tragic fate. Helen, daughter of Michael II, died in prison far from the island.

History and Conjecture

The waves of the invading East reached as far as the island; burst into these green valleys and groves. Corcyra stands as a boundary stone in the history of Turkish conquest for it did not reach farther east. Here it broke and fell, and the key to the Adriatic was held firm by the Venetians.

Under Venice she prospered—at least in forests; for the Venetians gave ten gold pieces for every grove of a hundred olive-trees planted, until when they left, it is said, the islanders possessed nearly two million trees.

Lithgow published an account of Corfu in 1632. It is as follows:

'Corfu is an island no less beautiful than invincible: it lieth in the Sea Ionean, the inhabitants are Greeks, and the Governors Venetians; this Ile was much honoured by Homer for the pleasant gardens of Alcino which were in his time. This Alcino was that Corcyrean poet who so benignly received Ulysses after his shipwracke, and of whom Ovid said:

> *Quid bifera Alconoi referam pomaria? Vos que*
> *Qui nunquam vacui prodistis in aethere rami.*
>
> *Why blaze I forth Alconoe's fertile soil*
> *And trees, from whence, all times they fruit recoyle?*

This Isle was given to the Venetians by the Corsicans [*sic*], Anno 1382, because they were exposed to all injuries in the world: It lieth like to a half moon, or half a circle east and north.

'The City Corfu, from which the Ile hath its name, is situate at the foot of a Mountain whereupon are builded two strong fortresses, and invironed with a rock. The one is called Fortezza Nova and the other Fortezza Vecchia. They are well governed and circumspectly kept, lest by the instigation of the one Captain the other should commit any treasonable effect. And for the same purpose the Governors of both castles, at their election before the senators of Venice are sworn; neither privately nor openly to have mutual conference; nor to write to one another for the space of two years, which is the time of their Government.

'The Castels are inaccesable and unconquerable, if that the keepers be loyal, and provided with natural and martial furniture. They are vulgarly called The Forts of Christendom, by the Greeks;

but more justly, The Strength of Venice; for if these forts were taken by the Turks, or by the Spaniard who would gladly have them, the trade of the Venetian merchants would be of none account; yea, the very means to overthrow Venice itself.'

Despite the slight inaccuracies Lithgow's sketch of the island is as charming and as fresh as a water-colour. The Corsicans are, of course, mythological—unless the word is a misprint for 'Corcyreans'; and at no time could the hillock upon which the old fort stands be called a mountain. But in its general particulars the account captures much of the charm of the place.

Earlier than Lithgow by about a decade Fynes Morison dedicated a small place in his *Itinerary* to a description of the island which deserves quotation. The year was 1596.

'On Sunday the 5th of May we did see the Mountain Fanon (and as I remember an Iland), three miles distant from the Iland Corfu, and upon the Greek shore beyond the Iland, we did see the most high mountains called Chimerae, inhabited by the Albanesi, who neither subject to the Turks nor Venetians, nor any other, do upon occasion rob all; and the Venetians, and the Kings of France, and especially of Spain, use to hire them in their wars.

'The Iland Corfu inhabited by Greeks is very fertile, yielding plenty of fruits, corn, wine, currants, and this haven is fortified with two Forts cut out off a Rock, namely, the old and the new Fort (which is more than a mile in circuit), both being very strong and held inexpugnable, so as the island is worthily reputed one of the Chief Keys of Christendom.'

2.10.37

The literati of 'The Partridge' have spent a great deal of time upon the etymological derivation of the word 'Corfu'. The current explanation that the Byzantine use of the word was related in some way to κὸρυφαι (meaning twin-peaked) is not entirely acceptable to Zarian though Theodore's more exacting scholarship appears to accept the idea. Any modern Greek dictionary will list κόρφος which means 'a gulf'; while research into the word Corcyra will give you the following: κέρκος (a tail, a handle); κὲρκουρος (a fish); and κερκὶς (a weaver's comb, a leg-bone, a fiddle-bow).

Each of us has his preference in this burning matter. Nimiec,

who is an unqualified cynic in all things concerning the Greek
language and character, chooses the latter as being most likely
because least logical. N. thinks that the gulf is the simplest and
most prosaic derivation. I prefer the figurative and visual derivation from a tail, because the island does taper away into a handle
at the southern end—as anyone can see by glancing at the map.
Zarian clings to the simple and fishy derivation, declaring that the
island has at all times been famous for its abundance of fish. 'You
will notice how carefully the wells are blessed by the priests against
the summer drought; have you ever seen them blessing the sea?'

Theodore prefers to remain beyond the range of all this inexact
and unfruitful scholarship. He merely shakes his head and sips his
yellow wine.

4.10.37

According to Diodorus, the Sicilian, Kerkura, the daughter of
Oceanus and Tethys was carried into the island by Neptune. Here
she bore the loved Phaex who ruled over it calling it Korkura.

Bochart derives the two names Scheria and Kerkyra from the
Phoenecian words 'scara' meaning 'commerce' and 'carcara'
meaning 'abundance'.

The island's fertility made it the favourite abode of green Ceres;
it was here she concealed the scythe with which the first Titians
were taught the art of husbandry. Hence the antique name
Drepani, a reaping hook.

It was also called Macria after the fair Macris who took refuge
here from the wrath of Juno.

5.10.37

As late as the third century B.C. a cave was shown to the superstitious where the marriage of Jason and Medea was said to have
taken place; as well as an altar to Apollo.

In the Naupactian Verses quoted by Pausanias they were said
to have returned here, and it is recorded that their son Mermeras
was killed while hunting on the opposite coast.

Short-sighted Procopius in the sixth century A.D. was shown the
petrified bark of Ulysses but his incredulity transformed it into a

fabric of stones dedicated to Jupiter Cassius by a wandering merchant.

6.10.37

Diodorus says that the island was originally colonized from some very remote part of the world; and indeed during the Trojan wars Corcyra was looked upon as a mysterious, semi-mythical island— a beautiful boundary-stone at the very edges of the known world. Enter Calypso's cave on the island north of Corcyra, and you will hear nothing but the faint bumping of the tides against the headland and the thin, shrill appeals of the gulls.

There are no Cyclopean remains in Corcyra; consequently you are free from the oppressive blood guilt of Tiryns—its blocks of hewn stone drenched with blood: of Mycaenae with its burial grounds choked with bodies, and the obsessive numbing drone of bees in the dark tomb of Agamemnon. You are still in a Latin world.

7.10.37

Temples were once numerous; Thucidides mentions temples to The Dioscori, Juno, and Alcinous; Jupiter Cassius was worshipped with sacrifices at Kassopi on the northern gulf.

9.10.37

The Greek permits himself one cerebral disturbance which from time immemorial has been capable of overturning the whole structure of the state: politics. Not the barren politics of abstractions and principles, but the warm cruel politics of the heart: hero-worship, the advancement of parties and personalities. In this alone we catch a glimpse of his bitter dualism of heart—an interior anarchy, which will not let him rest. I have been dipping into Jervis and wondering at the sameness of the general pattern; both in ancient and modern times it is the same impetus which carries affairs forward: arguments, obsessions, pride, panic, self-advancement.

'Mnasippus, bent on reducing the town by starvation. . . .'

'Being in need of money to pay his men Iphicrates attempted to ransome his numerous prisoners. . . .'

History and Conjecture

'Ctesicles attempted to restore order and unity.'

Yet the anecdotal material in the history of this one small island is all the richer for the variety of its detail.

14.10.37

Periander, tyrant of Corinth, gave it as a present to his brutish son Lycophron who became its ruler. For a long time past bitter quarrels had been breaking out between them; at last a reconciliation took place, and so great was Periander's relief that he wrote suggesting that they should exchange thrones. When the Corcyreans became aware of the intentions of the feared and detested father of Lycophron, they rose up in a panic and slew the son—which was, of course, the worst thing they could have done. In revenge for this Periander seized three hundred Corcyrean nobles who happened to be living in his domains and sent them as slaves to the dreadful Alyattes II. Fortunately, however, the ship bearing these unfortunates was blown into Samos by a north-wester, and the indignant Samiots risked the wrath of Periander by rescuing them.

15.10.37

'. . . Of the affairs of this period,' writes Jervis, 'little more than confused accounts remain. It appears from a fragment of Diodorus the Sicilian that not long subsequent to the battle of Ipsus, Cassander beseiged Corcyra by sea and by land, but he was obliged to raise the seige by Agathocles of Sicily himself who burnt the whole of the Macedonian Fleet and afterwards gave the island as a dowry to his daughter Lanassa, on her marriage with Pyrrhus, King of Epirus.

'Owing, however, to frequent intercourse with the East polygamy had become prevalent with Greek Princes; Pyrrhus was already married to two wives, one a Poeonian and the other an Illyrian Princess; and the attention he paid to them aroused the jealousy of the Syracusan lady. In order to revenge herself Lanassa retired to Corcyra.'

It is a landscape that does not nourish jealousies; certainly Lanassa's broken heart was soon mended; for she sent a proposal of marriage to the great Demetrius Poliorcetes himself. This Prince was so handsome that, it was said, no sculptor could be found whose art could do justice to him. His reaction to this proposal was at once thoughtful and deeply considered as befitted a prince and a political man. As he had recently concluded a non-aggression pact with the terrible Agathocles her father, he thought it would fit in very well, if he sealed the pact by marrying the heart-broken Lanassa. A story for moralists.

In Roman times, Agrippina touched here on her melancholy journey from Asia to Italy with the funeral urn of the noble Germanicus. Those few ashes hid all that was left of a world of ambition and pride and uprightness of character. She made only a short stay here '*to calm the agitation of a mind pierced to the quick*'.

17.10.37

Confused and out of key with their own lives Anthony and Octavia landed here from an imperial galley; he was on his way to Syria, while she had decided to return slowly to Rome—and to a world of favours as empty as his embraces. . . .

'A landscape for resolutions and partings,' says Zarian in an essay on famous visitors to Corcyra. 'A landscape which precipitates the inward crisis of lives as yet not fully worked out.' This is from a passage which describes the meeting of Cicero and Cato in the shadow of the fortress in 48 B.C.. The former was on his way to Italy to throw himself on Caesar's mercy; the latter 'not having yet despaired of the Commonwealth' was to set sail in company with Cneius Pompeius, for Africa.

19.10.37

Winter quarters for Consuls during the wars between Macedonia and Rome. The wind whitening the reedy stretches of Paleopolis and shrieking through the olive-groves of Perama. On the northern escarpment the seas pounding at Peristeri (Island of Turtle-Doves), and running white and yellow with the undertow of silt from the Butrinto estuary. Civil servants yawning away a winter over wood fires making inventories of fodder and shipping. 'In the last campaign between Pompey and Julius Caesar, the former increased his navy by the shipping of the isle; and had it occupied by the main body of the Fleet under M. Bibulus.'

History and Conjecture

Here Titus, Vespasian's son, watched with some impatience games given in his honour.

Geneseric, the ally of Attila, says Zarian, was a man who always trusted 'that the winds would bear him to a land the inhabitants of which had provoked the divine vengance'. He frequently visited this indented coastline in person with his pennoned fleet; and after the Vandals came the Goths under the terrible crooked Totila, to pillage and burn.

Having secured Rome, Totila had equipped 300 galleys manned by Goths and sent them down to conquer and ravage Greece. Justinian could only muster 50 sail and 5,000 men to oppose them. It was the Ice Age settling down on the Roman Empire; and for all the valour of Belisarius and Narses it could not be averted or withstood.

Somewhere in the lovely Valley Di Ropa you will come upon a small chapel-covered mound remarkable for the two superb umbrella-pines growing thereon. Above you to the left rises the single crag of Peleka above this expanse of green. To the right, almost hidden by the dense woodland, you will see a long curving drive lined with trees which aims slowly round upon a house with peeling green shutters. The cypresses lining the road are perhaps the most ancient in the island; their plumes are almost black, and near the ground are powdered by the fine golden summer dust. Mournful and unkept to the outward view, the house lies hidden from the main road.

This is the retreat of the Count D., and it is here that Zarian brought me one day to make the acquaintance of this celebrated recluse into whom the philosophic scepticism of a classical education had bitten so deeply. The old Count, a man of about sixty, was stocky and heavily built; he possessed a pair of remarkable eyes set in a head which was a little too big for his body. But the small hands and feet gave a distinctly Byronic cast to one's first impressions. When we first met it was some five or six years since he had first retired from the social life of the town to the calm of his country estate. In an island where loquacity and an over-burdening sense of hospitality are the norm it was natural that he should rank as a recluse and an eccentric. Zarian had made his acquaintance in the course of some negotiations about the rent of a town house he was intending to lease from him, and something in the temper of his mind (Zarian was incapable of conducting business except in terms of Neapolitan opera) must have appealed to the Count, for they became immediate and fast friends. And now we spend the first week-end of every month staying in the old house as guests.

27.10.37

Count D. is interesting. Unlike the majority of recluses he is a hospitable man. Comfortably off, fond of his cellar and his im-mense library, he is content to spend summer and winter beyond the limited range of town amusements and gossip. He shoots, assists at olive-pickings, and christens children; while the wine-yield of his property is a constant and delightful concern. The house and gardens were built by an Italian architect, so that though the walks are unkept and the trees unpruned the whole place retains some of the formal humanist charm of the Italian country house.

Here we spend our time in endless conversations. And here Zarian makes the effort of rising at dawn in order to verify the appositeness of the adjective 'rosy-fingered', which the Count main-tains to be the most exact as well as the most moving adjective in all literature. Despite several dawns Zarian has not yet agreed with his friend upon this subject.

The Count is a philosopher—'a philosopher', he will tell you deprecatingly in his faultless English or lapidary French, 'a philo-sopher who only sits and listens'. He speaks always with the most casual frankness about his own life and interests, his rather fine dark eyes fixed calmly upon his audience. He is filled with what Zarian (who is a born hero-worshipper and who finds a philoso-pher under every stone) calls 'a speculative calm'. It is rather the calm of one in whom the romantic is dead; and in whom the harder cutting-edge of experience has reached the inner man. Despite the sweetness and repose he is a prey to metaphysical incertitudes such as the artist only encounters; this you may guess from the fine sets of much-thumbed European philosophers which line his bedroom. 'Philosophy,' he said once, 'is a doubt which lives in one like hookworm, causing pallor and lack of appetite. Suddenly one day you awake and realize with complete certainty that ninety-five per cent of the activities of the human race—to which you supposed you belonged—have no relevance whatsoever for you. What is to become of you?'

On another occasion he said: 'I am popularly supposed to have retired here because of the death of my wife. It is convenient but not true. Two years before she died I woke up one morning, dressed very swiftly, and stood at the window of my room looking down on the harbour. I was visited by an extraordinary idea. I have had, I thought to myself, all the women I could want, and all the amusement I can possibly bear. Something has changed. I could not analyse the change—was it in me, or in the disposition of the world around me? It was a kind of detachment—an idea not born within the *conceptual* apparatus but lodged in the nervous system itself. I had become different as a person. Anyone else would have gone away and written a book about it; but I did not want to bring this personal discovery within the range of the conceptual apparatus, and thereby spoil it by consciousness. I retired, it is true, but you will see from my life as it lies around me, that what I am after is not the *interpretation* of the Principle of *x*, as I call it; but I wish to interpret the ordinary world of prescribed loyalties and little acts like shooting or lying or sleeping through the Principle. It is the oblique method of dealing with the platonic fire, after all, that betrays experience. Therefore if you come to me, like Zarian, and ask me why I am not writing down these discoveries, I can only reply that that is not what I mean by philosophy. I am enduring, and that is enough.'

It is for these remarkable flights that Zarian admires him so; and not the less for his gravity and the charm of his address. 'If only he would write a book,' says Zarian, the thirsty literary man, 'it would be a work of genius.' Then he adds rather more slowly: 'And if he can live without the thought of suicide. . . .'

But the Count has, by an imaginative detour, avoided the impasse in which people too heavily endowed with sensibility or the need for expressing it, find themselves. The old house with its Venetian family portraits and tarnished silver radiates an absolute calm. Greek terra cottas lie piled in dusty cupboards— broken jars and oil-dips, all relics of the plough from this fertile valley.

We dine late by candlelight; light almost as yellow as the moon outside the great windows of the dining-room; portraits of Venetian ancestors stare pallidly at us from the walls in their mouldering frames. The floors are full of dry-rot.

After the dinner the Count takes up a branch of candles and leads the way to the wine-covered terrace by the white southern wall on which the dapple of leaves silhouetted by moonlight stand out unmoving. Here we sit and talk away the greater part of the night. In the silences between our sentences we can hear the oranges dropping from the trees in the orchard—dull single thuds upon the mossy ground. The marble table is wet with dew. An owl cries, and the watchdogs at the lodge grumble and shake their chains.

The Count smokes his home-made cigarettes in a short bone holder, stained with nicotine. Relaxing, and spreading out his hands against the moonlight as if to warm them at its white fire, he begins to talk. I have wasted all these words on describing the Count in the hope of isolating that quality in him which is so admirable and original, and when he begins to talk I grasp at once what it is. He is the possessor of a literary mind completely uncontaminated by the struggle to achieve a technique; he lacks the artifice of presentation, the corrupting demon of *form*. It is a mind with the pollen still fresh upon it.

While we sit here Ourania the heavily made but beautiful peasant girl comes out in her bare feet, the corner of her blue headdress gripped modestly between her white teeth, and arranges glasses of Visino before us; 'Would'st give me water with berries in't?' says the Count reflectively—'have I never told you that Corcyra is Prospero's island? This', he indicates the glass in which Ourania has placed a spoonful of dark viscous raisin jam, 'is one of the links in my chain of reasoning. I cannot think that the scholars would support me, but you, my friend,' turning to Zarian, 'you would take a little pleasure in the knowledge that Shakespeare was thinking of Corcyra when he wrote *The Tempest*. Who knows? Perhaps he even visited it.'

It is the kind of opening which Zarian loves so much. His silver hair gleams in the moonlight. Taking his spectacles from his pocket, as if the better to follow the Count's reasoning, he places them on his nose and says: 'Now then, Count. Defend this contention.'

The Count has taken a small silver-hilted pencil from the pocket of his cardigan and is busy tracing meaningless little shapes on the marble table. He dusts some specks of cigarette ash from his clothes, and writes the word SYCORAX before Zarian. 'Look,' he says, 'Caliban's mother, the mysterious blue-eyed hag who owned the island upon which Prospero was cast—her name is almost too obvious an anagram for CORCYRA.' He pauses for an instant and raises his eyes to Zarian's eager face. He is unable to resist smiling at his friend. 'Shall I go on?'

'You will remember the Principle of *x* of which I was speaking? It struck me that perhaps in the work of the great artists I might find this outpost of the sensibility charted. In the course of my reading I stumbled upon *The Tempest*. I found what I was looking for in Prospero, but while I was reading the play I was struck by a few elements in it of a peculiarly Ionian nature. If you lose patience with the idea please tell me and I will stop. First of all, the shipwreck. Prospero's Island it is abundantly clear is somewhere off the main route between Tunis and Naples. I propose to disregard the claims for Lampedusa and Malta; and I think that if you observe the colouring of the text you will see that it is peculiarly Greek. Think of Caliban's imprecation "A south-west blow on ye, And blister ye all o'er", and reflect to yourself whether this south-wester is not the worst evil that could befall an Ionian—sirocco weather. Then, to go a little further with Caliban; he enumerates the qualities of the isle as "The fresh springs, brine-pits, barren place and fertile". I ask myself here whether the Venetian salt-pans in the south of the island might not have been in his mind.' The Count says this with a singular and deprecating sweetness; I can see that he anticipates Zarian's protest. 'Zante has also a claim under that head. There was a prodigious trade with Zante during Elizabethan times; Lithgow mentions the currants which the English used in their puddings; and even if you read mere teachers of languages like Hollyband you find an unself-conscious reference to the island—proving that to the average Elizabethan merchant Zante was already well known. And of course the salt-pans of Zante would be better known.'

The Count nods patiently. 'Perhaps too well known, not quite mysterious enough to furnish the imaginative background for the desert island of *The Tempest*. We are on delicate ground. Yet you must agree that the colouring is Mediterranean—"And thy broom groves, whose shadow the dismissed bachelor loves, being lass-lorn; thy pole-clipped vineyard and thy sea-marge, sterile and rocky-hard". What do you say to that, my friend?'

Zarian is too patently seduced by the idea to say anything at all; in his mind I can see he is planning a whole article on this remarkable idea. He sits impatiently in his chair and waits for the Count to speak. The latter takes a turn up and down the terrace trying to remember further quotations to support this delightful fantasy. At each Zarian's enthusiasm grows.

'I must,' he says at last, 'I must drink to this noble discovery. Count, this is a memorable addition to our knowledge about Corcyra.'

'Then,' says the Count, in a voice mellow with pleasure and a certain triumph, 'let us drink a glass of Visino—which I have christened Caliban's Wine. "Water with berries in't", is, to my mind, not coffee, as most of the commentators would have it, but βύσινο—this unusual Ionian drink. Your health, my dear Zarian.'

The health is unduly prolonged in a bottle of red Kastellani wine, while Zarian plunges deeper into the maze of surmise and conjecture. 'We cannot be certain whether Shakespeare ever came here,' says the Count, 'but we can ask ourselves two things. First, who is the "Well-wishing adventurer" who is described as "setting forth" in the dedication to the sonnets? The second is this: Shakespeare was too well known to be the victim of an open piracy by 1609. But if he were *out of the country* it is possible that Mr. Thorpe might have had the courage to print the sonnets. *The Tempest* was written in 1611, they say.'

At this point, Theodore, who always retires formidably to bed at nine-thirty, puts down his massive volume of medical lore, blows out his candle and comes to the window above our heads. He receives Zarian's information about Shakespeare's visit with sceptical good humour, remarks on the clearness of the night. Looking towards the west you can see a strip of glittering sea drawing a line between two black olive-groves. Small breathless eddies of air come to us across the valley. Theodore sniffs appreciatively and says: 'Jasmine,' before bidding us good night and withdrawing his bearded head from the window. The three of us walk down across the lawn and through the orchard towards the little circular Rotonde which houses the battered statue of a Roman nymph. 'I trust', says the Count, 'that your wives are not offended with me for refusing to invite them to these meetings. If you permit me to say so, women tire me. Their presence introduces an atmosphere of politeness and favouritism; they will discuss poetry like angels until they notice a mirror in the corner of the room. They lack the magnanimity of the male mind.'

From this small hillock the prospect stretches away—vineyard, orchard and wood, with its insinuating lines: to the last bluff line of limestone crags beyond which the sea coils and uncoils its silver meshes. From Paleocastrizza the fishermen are setting out with their coracles of straw and wood.

'One sleeps lightly these moonlight nights,' says the Count. We pass an arbour in which, sitting like statues at a deal table, we see a peasant and his wife. Their low voices sound clear and rich upon the breathless night. 'To-morrow we shall ride down to the sea together. I have a horse for you each.'

And so quietly back to the house, and through the great doorway. The candles have burnt down to their guttering ends. The Count distributes them like blessings. We make our way to our several rooms in silence.

Closing the shutters against the staring moon, I pick up a book from the pile lying on top of a cupboard in the corner of a room; it is a commonplace book, full of entries in the fine small hand of the Count. More than half of it is given up to accounts, which are entered in Italian. There is a list of Greek peasant proverbs, a rough drawing of a strip of coastline over the legend 'Dodona's Shrine?', two designs for sailing-boats, and the following quotation:

History and Conjecture

'Lingering perdition, worse than any death
Can be at once, shall step by step attend
You, and your ways, whose wraths to guard you from,
Which here in this most desolate isle, else falls
Upon your heads, is nothing but heart's sorrow,
And a clear life ensuing.'

28.10.37

Goodisson records the existence of a 'fine quarry of marble under the western peak of St. Salvador, of a very fine grain, and well adapted to the use of statuary'. Niko has made us a garden table and seat from this lovely stuff, which is of a deep salmon pink and shot with lines of rust-red.

29.10.37

William Goodisson, A.B., whose 'Historical and Topographical' essay on the island was published in 1822 is sometimes interesting, but often dull and moribund. He charms us most when he is most scientific—and surely no more charming feat than his measurement of the 'Chemical Properties of Sappho's Leap' (in Leukada) could be imagined. 'Chemical Analysis of Sappho's Leap' would make a charming sub-title for the following piece of information: 'External properties: of a clear sugar whiteness, with a few glimmering points in the internal fracture resembling that of fine loafsugar. Sp. Gravity. 2·263.'

2.11.37

Cressida has left her name and her legend to grace the reedfringed edges of the Hyallic Lake; but the force of the stream seems much diminished since 1822, when the speed of the current is said to have turned a mill at 300 metres from the source.

7.11.37

The discovery that Judas Iscariot has a direct connection with Corcyra has provided a great deal more grist to Zarian's mill. Theodore happened to be discussing a first edition of Petrarch which has just been discovered in the uncatalogued jumble of rarer MSS. belonging to the Library with the curator, when the name of Pietro Della Valle was mentioned. The quotation, as it appears in Zarian's essay, is as follows: 'Here also lives a man reputedly of the race of Judas. . . . I remember a servant of ours who resided at Corfu affirming that some of the Apostate's descendants still existed there, and that a house he inhabited was pointed out.' The date was 1614.

Walking through the verminous and crooked streets of the Hebraica with Theodore we discuss the problem from all its angles. The cobbled alleys are slippery with excrement. The little shops, made for the most part of the flimsiest materials, are worm-eaten and decayed. Yet counters groan with cheap dress materials, mounds of sweets, and everywhere the tap of shoemakers' hammers emphasizes the gnome-like quality of the place. It is natural, of course, that until to-day we have never noticed the name of Theodore's shoemaker: ISCARIOTES. It is painted in lopside capitals on a sagging board. The man himself is a deaf mute with some of the lowering gloomy aspect of Dr. Faustus. He works from a skilful and pedantic set of brown-paper patterns which Theodore has cut out for him. The skin of his face and hands is ingrained with dirt and cobbler's wax. He never smiles. The hair on his face grows high up on the cheekbones so that, unshaven, he seems to be suffering from powder-markings—as if from the discharge of the gun. 'His eyebrows', says Zarian with disappointment, 'do not meet in the middle.' (Popular superstition suggests that this is one of the signs of the Evil Eye.)

Nevertheless the occasion is too good a one to miss, and Zarian draws his notebook from his pocket. Just how to interview a deaf mute, however, is a problem which none of us can solve. Iscariotes can only move his pinkish tongue in his mouth with a faint snake-like composure; he can groan through his nose. And to complete the record of our misfortunes he is illiterate. He appears to have no family, and nobody in the surrounding shops knows anything about him except that he has been working at his little skin-covered bench for many years. Voluble and excited, Zarian falls into the Venetian dialect which the Jews in this quarter use among themselves, but without result. Iscariotes shakes his head and attempts a laugh; he does this noiselessly by inflating his throat as a snake its hood—until you can see his pink tongue moving among the yellowed stumps of teeth. It is rather a failure.

Yet later in the alcove of 'The Partridge' Zarian recovers his composure as he proceeds to give us an account of the Jewish Colony of Corcyra.

When Benjamin of Tudela visited the island in 1160 he found only one Jew there—a dyer.

In 1571 Venice expelled the Jews from her dominions; yet by some chance the Jews of Corcyra were left undisturbed. In 1760 they were a colony 1,171 strong, while when the first French warships arrived to claim the island fortress for France some 2,000 were recorded in the census figures. By 1860 the colony numbered some 6,000 souls according to British computations.

Yet where does the ceremony of casting out Judas originate? At eleven o'clock on Good Friday every year, the unwary visitor is suddenly terrified out of his wits by the discharge of masses of crockery into the streets, pots, pans, and cauldrons, while the air is made hideous by the banging of pistols. This is supposed to be a ceremony for the casting out of Judas; and the banging and yelling continue (with pauses for refreshment) throughout the day.

The Hebraica still guards its isolation and its language, and its members play little or no part in the life of the island. Yet the age of persecutions is by no means over; Zarian has observed how during Easter Week you will never see a Jew outside the confines of their settlement. But the finest wedding embroideries come from the Hebraica, and the greatest range of pottery and the tinsmith's wares are to be seen there.

'On the 13th February 1386 Corfu was once more a Venetian possession. . . . On the 20th of May the people of Corfu, at a public meeting to appoint five ambassadors to submit to the Venetian senate, for confirmation of the treaty already made, had included a Jew in the Embassy named David Somos. . . .'

Howell in his *Travells* mentions the Venetian dialect which they speak even to-day.

10.11.37

'To Napoleon,' says Zarian, who rejoices in great names, 'Corfu was the keystone to an Empire in the East. If he had been exiled here instead of in St. Helena there is no knowing but that his proud stony heart might have been softened.'

History and Conjecture

In his diary the French conqueror wrote: 'Venice must fall to those to whom we give the Italian continent, but meanwhile we will take its vessels, strip its arsenal, destroy its bank, and keep Corfu and Ancona. . . .' 'With Malta and Corfu we should soon be masters of the Mediterranean.' And later, in a letter to Talleyrand he added: 'I think that henceforth the chief maxim of the French Republic should be never to give up Corfu, Zante, etc.'

In 1815 the Ionian Islands were created a single, free and independent state under the sole protection of Britain; and the era of the larger lunacy began. For the curious, the hyperborean prose of Napier will provide an effective counterblast to any suggestion that British colonies are, in the nature of things, perfectly governed. Yet Adams brought the town water, and the remains of the solid and beautiful roads built by the British still remain. Solomos was accepted and even petted. The Earl of Guilford, surely one of the most remarkable eccentrics of the last century, was persuaded to relinquish Ithaca as a home for his Ionian Academy, and to found the University of Corfu in 1823. The relief of the elegant Jervis White-Jervis is exhaled in every line. 'What would it have been,' he writes, 'if Lord Guilford had succeeded in carrying out his object of establishing the University at Ithaca. Visionary ideas of academical groves and of the birthplace of Ulysses do not form men to be useful citizens; and from one student who would have been sent from there, a hundred men would have been turned out upon the world with their ideas confined to a barren rock and a few goats.'

16.11.37

Sitting in the shade of the olive-trees overlooking the dazzle of Mouse Island set in its burnished emerald sea, the Count discourses amiably upon the British occupation, with that quiet mordant turn of voice, while Zarian and Theodore feast upon green olives and white cheese. It is one of our many afternoons in search of lore; we have been scouring the lovely hill of Analypsis for traces of the Temple to Neptune, supposed to have been noted by British Naval officers towards the end of the last century. Now dropping down through the silver olive-groves we have come to Canoni, where Lord Kitchener complete with side-whiskers and

85

moustache keeps a small tavern; and where Edwardian ginger-beer, made after an Edwardian recipe, is served in little stone bottles with a marble for a cork. This is known to the islanders as 'Tsit-Tsin Beera' and provides a convenient point of departure for the Count, who has been supplementing Zarian's store of anecdotes by an account of how Mr. Gladstone and the Bishop of Paxo, in an access of reciprocal politeness (in an attempt to kiss each others' hands) banged their skulls together during a very solemn ceremony and were only restored by a bottle of ginger-beer such as we are now consuming.

'People in search of the vanished Imperial culture of England would find very little in Corfu: and that little curious. I do not speak about prevailing attitudes of mind; we have, of course, a certain number of Greeks educated abroad, who ape the English. I have inherited, for example, from my family—which once governed here under the British—a strong taste for good manners and fair dealing as a living part of my *amour-propre*, not as independent virtues of character. It is the great difference between French culture and British; the British have no character—they depend upon very highly developed principles. It is convenient because they do not have to think. But apart from this Britain's legacy to Corcyra is an odd one; you have seen, have you not, in the dirty little alleys between the Hebraica and the port, a strange symbol chalked upon the walls? No? Wander into the alleys, and you will be suddenly surprised to see the wickets and bails of the slum cricketer everywhere; you will suddenly think you are in Stepney.' Cricket lives on as independently as the patron saint. It is a mysterious and satisfying ritual which the islanders have refused to relinquish; and every year in August when the British Fleet comes in, cricket enjoys her festival. A ripple of anticipation runs through the groups of dawdlers on the sunny esplanade; and the two cricket clubs of the town can be seen practising ferociously at the nets on the hard red earth, in the shadow of Schulemberg's statue. Groups of peasants, mysteriously drawn by their anticipation, stand in the shadow of the trees talking and observing. Meanwhile the British battleships ride squatly in the harbour and their fussy pinnaces throw up lines of ripples which, hours later, will disturb your Father Nicholas at his lobster-pots off St. Stephano and cause him mightily to curse 'the cuckold British'. When the news comes that the challenge to a cricket match has been received, there is an audible sigh of relief and pleasure which runs the length of the town. At once a profound clamour of activity breaks out; a matting pitch is laid in the centre of the esplanade; a marquee is hastily run up; the Ministry of Supply in Athens receives an incoherent telegram asking it to obtain from the British Legation the recipe for rock cakes, which has somehow been mislaid once again this year. The British Consul is to be seen in morning clothes. All British residents of the town gain face in a remarkable way. Some receive presents of fruit and poultry—for this is after all, not far short of a Saint's Day. And when the teams, eleven aside, and clad in their ceremonial white, meet on the ground for the toss, excitement and admiration reach their height. Peasants come in to town and take the afternoon off to sit under the trees on those uncomfortable café chairs, gravely applauding whenever the specialists (who sit in the marquee among the naval representatives and the consuls, and whose role is that of officiating priests) think fit to give them the cue. The British chaplain, who looks like nothing so much as a half-drowned blackbeetle rescued from a water-butt, sits in the midst of the distinguished guests, confirming by his presence the religious quality of the ritual. Everybody except St. Spiridion himself appears to be present. And in the evening, by time-honoured custom, a British Band in brilliant coats, marches to the bandstand and delights the crowds by its martial flourishes until the last light dies away and the fireflies come flashing out in their thousands. For the benefit of Zarian I must add here that the terminology of cricketers in Corcyra has suffered with the passage of years. In some curious way the cry 'How's that?' has come to mean 'Out' while 'runs' are known as 'ronia'. The bails on the wickets are known as 'rollinia' and the drive is called 'pallia'. A yorker and a leg glide are known respectively as a 'Primo Salto' and a 'Sotto Gamba'; there are a few other small anomalies but I forget them for the moment. But while we are on the question of words I recall two English words which have been baptized into modern Greek. One is the verb 'to cost' which is used with a conventional verb-ending and pronounced very much as it is in English; the other is an English draper's measure 'the peak' which

has become 'pika'. When you add to all this the private manufacture of apple chutney you have, I think, exhausted the subject of
British cultural traces in the Ionian.

26.11.37

Viscount Kirkwall, who has written what the Count calls 'the
most exasperatingly friendly and honest book' about the British
occupation, captures the Victorian atmosphere of sidewhiskers and
sideboots in a disarming manner. He records the dislike of the
Ionians for their bluff rulers—a dislike which has changed since
their departure into a nostalgic love and admiration. Set in this
décor of cypress-grove and lake, his characters move creaking with
gentility and imperial self-satisfaction. He records the paper-
chases and the tea-parties in this outlandish corner of the world;
the splash of red coats moving under the fortress to the sound of
bugles—beaten thin as gold by the winds across the straits. He
records with complete fidelity the humours and trials of guardian-
ship by an Empire which has never cared to condescend to its
subjects by the exercise of understanding; but confirms them in its
love through an exasperating solidity and shy humour.

'On the 9th of May there was a sham siege and assault carried
on in the island of Vido; where a good luncheon was laid out in
the tents for the officers and visitors. The affair, tho' well arranged,
was on a small scale; as only part of the garrison of Corfu rein-
forced for the occasion the troops at Vido. But from the picturesque nature of the ground the attack and defence manœuvres
formed a pleasing spectacle which even ladies could appreciate.
The interest was increased by the fact that some degree of risk was
incurred by the troops; as the scaling-ladders employed in the
attack did not quite reach to the top of the ditch. But as regarded
this difficulty no accident occurred. An artilleryman, however,
was, by the hasty discharge of a gun, accidentally thrown into the
ditch of the principal work.'

29.11.37

When the Ionian Islands were ceded to Greece, and the evacua-
tion began, the Ionians were horrified to learn that extensive de-
molitions were to be carried out on the forts. As they had con-

tributed in taxation about two-thirds of the total cost of building the fortresses, they were naturally bitter. Kirkwall, who showed some considerable sympathy for the Greeks, and for the Corcyreans in particular, is indignant too. His detailed description of the demolition work being carried out during that rainy February of 1864 is a brilliant piece of work.

To the English colony it was as exciting as a prolonged firework display. 'On the afternoon of Tuesday, 29th March, numbers of English ladies and gentlemen, in spite of wind, heavy rain, and rolling seas, crossed over to Vido in order to witness from the keep the destruction of the strong Lunette battery to the west of the island.'

To the Ionians, however, all this earnest blowing up of 'notable ramps, earthworks, embrasures' only underlined the bitterness of the departure. One disgusted Ionian is recorded to have remarked to Kirkwall as a puff of smoke and a jet of falling clods marked the blowing up of another 'notable' rampart: 'I wish Lord Roosel were on top of it.'

'The earlier mines', writes Kirkwall, 'were fired by long trains of powder laid on the ground in furrows and slow burning fuses. But after the arrival of a Voltaic Battery from England the affair was arranged in the Scientific Manner which suited better to this Age of Wonders.'

The discreet picnics among the olive-groves, the memoranda, the protocols, the bustles, sidewhiskers, long top-boots, tea-cosies, mittens, rock-cakes, chutney, bolus, dignity, incompetence, book-keeping, virtue, church bazaars; you will find traces of all of them if you look deeply enough. The flash of red hunting coats through the olive-groves as the officers galloped over the island on their dangerous paper-chases; the declarations of love among the cypresses, the red-faced sportsmen setting out for Albania. Big Tom, Adams, Leech, and 'Fusty' Andrews; Lockler, Jones, and Jervis White-Jervis. Dr. Anstead fussily visiting these 'embayed seas' to record the lamentable venality of the islanders. Edward Lear's gloomy pictures of Perama and the Hyallic Gulf. Caught once and for all and absorbed into the atmosphere and line of the landscape with its arbours, mountains, and Byronic moonlight; preserved in a style of moustache among the peasants, or in the top-hatted mommets of the Karaghiozis pantheon, or in the fragmentary touching love of the small urchins who will run crying beside the antiquated horse-carriages which no taxis can ever oust, offering 'flowers for the Englishman's lady' in accents no German or Frenchman has ever heard. Nothing has been lost of England's inner accent; yet the forts lie empty of ordnance and cannon-balls. The battleships come now as visitors. And Turnock's Royal Hotel where Anstead met with 'food, civility, and moderate prices' has left no trace behind it.

1.12.37

The French burned the Golden Book in which the names of the Venetian families were inscribed, and the aristocracy died in the flames to be reborn, phoenix-like, in titles stiff and unreal as old brocade.

The British did their best to reinstate the aristocratic tradition— as the Count would say 'by abstract principles'.

When Britain left the abrupt fierce history of the island seemed to cease, and the gradual decay of communications and facilities made it more than ever remote, mysterious, and hard to reach. The landscape reverted to its own prolix disordered pattern. The stout roads have remained to this day; and the water-supply of the town, despite periodic hitches, still operates as smoothly as when Adams first devised and carried out its building. But there is one English eccentricity remarked by the natives which the Count has missed; the English demand for houses with lavatories. An 'English' house in the island, has come to mean a house with a lavatory; and the landlord of such a house will charge almost double the ordinary rent for so remarkable an innovation. Bathrooms are even rarer and are considered a dangerous and rather satanic contrivance. For the peasants a bath is something you are sometimes forced to take by the doctor as a medicinal measure; the idea of cleanliness does not enter into it. Theodore often quotes the old peasant who reverently crossed himself when shown the fine tiled bathroom at the Count's country house and said: 'Pray God, my Lord, that you will never need it.'

History and Conjecture

Nimiec has an anecdote, unsavoury if illustrative, which should find a place in the appendix to Harington's *Metamorphoses*; he arrived at a fishing village in Merlera on one of his fishing jaunts, and was housed in a small cottage with an earth lavatory, primitive and so full of flies that he drew the attention of his host to its condition. His host said briskly, 'Flies? Of course there are flies. If you could do as we all do and wait until just before the midday meal you would not find a fly in the lavatory. They all come round to the kitchen.'

3.1.38

Jervis states that there are only three considerable historians of the island, but if one must speak the truth, there is only one history of the island written in the true Corcyrean spirit, gay, mendacious, and self-assured. This is by Andrea Di Marmora, who published it in Venice in 1670. His record of Corcyra's history is justly considered a standard work by Zarian. 'I confess', says Jervis, 'to have been rather startled when I read in this author that the Romans conquered Britain and defeated the Parthians owing to the assistance received from the Corcyreans, but there was a certain charm in reading the history of Rome in such a new light.'

4.1.38

The Saint does not seem to have played a great part in the age of British Protection; it is presumed that he was sulking since on one occasion the Governor (a dull and brutish fellow) refused the islanders the use of a military band to celebrate Spiridion's festival.

Yet I am happy to find in Kirkwall that a certain Colonel Wright of the Royal Artillery, set matters right with the old fellow. He obtained leave for the saluting battery in the fort to remain untouched as, says Kirkwall, 'he thought it hard that the Corfiots should be denied the pleasure of saluting St. Spiro'.

There is no statue to Colonel Wright on the esplanade. But it is to be hoped that his name has been passed up by Spiridion for inscription in the Golden Book—not of St. Mark, but of St. Peter.

5.1.38

Shooting rabbits on the island of Vido my brother records the following conversation with a man about to embark in a rowing-boat for the mainland.

'Good morning.'

'Good morning.'

'Where are you from?'

'From the prison.'

'Where are you going?'

'Home. I get every week-end off.'

'What is your sentence?'

'A life sentence. I am a murderer.'

Vido was once nobly wooded; but the French cut down all the trees in order to facilitate military operations. The prison is a pleasant white-washed building standing back from the sea. The prisoners themselves keep up a steady trade in little carved objects of wood and beaten metal; workmanship of a stylized Byzantine kind, but sensitive and pleasant in its crude way.

6.1.38

The flying-boats of Imperial Airways have discovered Govino, where the earthworks and embrasures of the Venetian port sink yearly deeper in the silt. Here in the shadow of Pantocratoras the big-bellied Shorts circle and hover until their keels suddenly rip open the emerald lake surface, and the long shavings of water curl up on each side. Spiro is the favourite taxi-driver of the pilots; they like his Brooklyn drawl, his boasting, his coyness; he combines the air of a chief conspirator with a voice like a bass viol. His devotion to England is so flamboyant that he is known locally as Spiro Americanos. Prodigious drinker of beer, he resembles a cask with legs; coiner of oaths and roaring blasphemies, he adores little children, and never rides out in his battered Dodge without two at least sitting beside him listening to his stories. We never see 'his pilots'—as he calls them—yet one of them lives in our memory as the author of a gesture in keeping with the spirit of the island. One of these English boys on the homeward trip takes back a bunch of Corcyrean flowers for his wife; at four in the morning, an hour before the departure, he and Spiro drive out to Canoni and gather flowers in the light of the headlamps from that dew-drenched sward above Mouse Island. With the first light of dawn he is in the air, heading for England, with his wet bunch of narcissi or grave asphodel. It is the kind of little devotion that touches the raw heart of Spiro as he pants and grunts up the slopes of Canoni, his big fists full of wet flowers, and his sleepy mind thinking of the English girl who to-morrow will touch this lovely evidence of the island's perpetual spring. Spiro is dead.

VI

Landscape with Olive Trees

10.1.38

Dominant in a landscape full of richer greens, the olive is for the peasant both a good servant and a hard master. In the good olive year whose harvest stretches across from January to May, the whole country population is busy attending to the tree which provides the island with its staple diet—olive oil.

Throughout the spring months, through the gales of March and the hard sunspots of April, the tireless women are out with their soft wicker hampers gathering the fruit as it falls. In the other islands the fruit is beaten from the tree and the tree itself pruned; but in Corcyra this has been, for hundreds of years, considered harmful. Prolix in its freedom therefore the olive takes strange shapes; sometimes it will swell and burst open, ramifying its shoots until a whole clump of trees seems to grow out of the breast of the parent; in some places (there is one particular grove between Kouloura and Kassopi) the trees grow tall and slender, with bodies not rough, but of a marvellous platinum-grey, and branches aerial and fine of attitude. In the northern crags again the olive crouches like a boxer; its roots undermine roads; its skin is rough and wormy; and its pitiful exhausted April flowering is like an appeal for mercy against the conspiracy of rock and heat.

There is no estate without its oil magazine—a low building with stamped earthen floor which houses the presses and all the machinery of the trade. It is here that the long lines of coloured women come, bearing their baskets full of the sloe-shaped fruit, now covered in bloom. And here they stand, gorgeous as birds, they shake the rain from their dresses and receive their dole of bread and piercing garlic.

Built up against the wall of the magazine lie the cold stone bunkers which slowly brim with the fruit; while monstrous in the

Landscape with Olive Trees

shadows stands the massive and primitive mill. This has a stone bed with a gutter about three feet high. From its centre a beam supports a granite millstone. A smaller beam standing at right angles to this can be harnessed to the neck of a pony which supplies the millstone's power.

On wet days when a big wood fire is built at which the women can dry themselves as they come in from olive-gathering, the shadows leap and flap against the gloom of the archways, throwing into sudden relief the strings of onions and tobacco hanging from the roof, the unruffled chickens lying in the straw, the weaving-loom, and perhaps the sagacious evil face of the billy-goat munching in a corner.

The olive-gathering is an all-weather business; in the blinding February storms you hear the little hard berries dropping to the ground, and, if you happen to be standing on high ground looking southward you can see the visible track of the north wind as it strikes the valley, turning the olive trees inside out—so that they change from green to silver and back to green. Under the shelter of archway and wall the women stoop in circles steadily filling their hampers while the rain rattles like small-shot in the leaves about them and the first thirsty wild flowers stir in the cold ground under their feet.

But the olive-tree has hardly suited its internal economy to its position, for its attenuated white flowering commences in April, just when it is most occupied with the ripening of its fruit: so that if its previous year's blossom has been prolific, it has hardly the strength to blossom again. Its crop is irregular, and the lean years for the harvesters are very lean indeed. Bread and oil as a diet hardly leaves any margin for thrift.

After the first pressing in the mill-bed the men come with their wide-mouthed baskets and gather up the magma, piling its greyish mass into a wooden press; the pony, whose efforts at the millstone are now no longer necessary, is unharnessed and turned loose in the paddock. Taking up the long wooden lever, the men begin to screw at the pulp, helping the oil away if the weather is cold, by pouring boiling water upon it. As the pressure becomes stronger, they fasten a rope to a sort of primitive windlass, and give the creaking structure their whole weight. It is like the birth of something in the gloom of the great magazine; their groans echo through the cypress floors of the house. The windlass creaks. The fowls cluck nervously about the feet of the men. Appreciatively sitting in the great fireplace with the light playing upon his beard, the abbot of the local monastery lends moral support as he sips his glass of wine.

The oil itself spurts dirtily in the stone gutters and slips drop by drop into the underground stone tanks where it will be left to settle itself into purity; while the madder coloured acid refuse is run off into the gutters—where its pungent smell and the scorched herbage of its course are familiar characteristics of the landscape.

After many settlings in the various stone tanks the oil is considered pure enough to send to the town to the bulk dealers, poured into leather skins, which bobble and gulp, it is loaded into carts which rumble slowly off down the circuitous paths to Corfu. Bright and greasy in the sunlight the skins jog hideously together like so many truncated corpses.

The cakes of the refuse, now dried brown and stiff, and empty of juice, are stacked in the dry corners of the magazine, to be used later for fuel. Broken up they burn with a subdued smouldering warmth, and added to wood and coal, give our winter stove fuel enough to carry us through the three worst months.

Though the olive is an undependable friend its role never varies; dipped into it, the coarse peasant bread tastes dense and foul—yet the children of the fishermen have warm brown skins and dazzling white teeth. Everything is cooked in it. And it is only poetic justice to observe that every saint's shrine has lamps which are replenished by the offering of the poor, who have slaved nearly the whole year round in varying weather to gathering the yield of the tree.

The whole Mediterranean—the sculptures, the palms, the gold beads, the bearded heroes, the wine, the ideas, the ships, the moonlight, the winged gorgons, the bronze men, the philosophers —all of it seems to rise in the sour, pungent taste of these black olives between the teeth. A taste older than meat, older than wine. A taste as old as cold water.

The olive in Corcyra is the smallholder's pride, and in the wooded parts of the island land values are usually computed on the basis of the number of olive-trees. It is usual for the larger

Landscape with Olive Trees

proprietors to let out the season's oil crop to the peasant living on the property, who works the crop and receives half the oil in return. But in the poorer villages holdings can amount to as little as two or three trees—and prospective property speculators take great care when buying a piece of land, to find out who owns the olive-trees, as their possession confers right of way.

14.1.38

Abstemious in the matter of drinks, the Greeks produce their own light wines and cognacs in abundance. Yet during our whole stay here we have seen a drunk person not more than once; and more endearing still, we have discovered that these people have so delicate a palate as to be connoisseurs of cold water. The glass of water appears everywhere; it is an adjunct to every kind of sweetmeat, and even to alcohol. It has a kind of biblical significance. When a Greek drinks water he *tastes* it, and pressing it against the palate, savours it. The peasants will readily tell you which wells give the sweetest water, while even the townspeople retain a delicate taste in water, and are able to recognize the different sources from which the little white town handcarts (covered in green boughs) are replenished.

Two days before Christmas we climbed the dizzy barren razorback of Pantocratoras to the monastery from which the whole strait lay bare, lazy and dancing in the cold haze. Lines of dazzling water crept out from Butrinto, and southward, like a beetle on a plate, the Italian steamer jogged its six knots towards Ithaca. Clouds were massing over Albania, but the flat lands of Epirus were frosty bright. In the little cell of the warden monk, whose windows gave directly upon the distant sea, and the vague rulings of waves to the east, we sat at a deal table and accepted the most royal of hospitalities—fresh mountain walnuts and pure water from the highest spring; water that had been carried up on the backs of women in stone jars for several hundred feet.

15.1.38

During the last summer visit to the Count D. we attended a ceremony which furnished the seed for a whole train of arguments about pagan survivals, which have since been incorporated in one

Landscape with Olive Trees

of Theodore's many unpublished monographs. The Count was half-way down the avenue of cypress trees when we came upon him, carrying in his hand a beautiful Venetian dish, full of something which only Theodore recognized as Colyva—the offering to the dead. 'You will perhaps walk with me,' said the Count, turning aside after his usual greetings, 'and assist me. I am making a small reverence to a cousin of mine who died two years ago to-day.' Noticing Zarian's hungry eye upon the dish (for our walk had been a long and dusty one) he smiled and said: 'It is a peasant custom still—and descended from who knows what pagan rite.' He removed the lid for us to look at the contents. 'Pomegranate seeds, wheat, pine-nuts, almonds and raisins, all soaked in honey. Here, it really tastes rather nice. Try some.' Together we walked with him through the wood, following the bridle-paths, until we came to the small chapel, surrounded by tall cypresses. The Count undid the heavy iron padlock which secured the door to what appeared to be the family vault. The gloom was intense, and the shadow thrown by the cypresses gave it a greenish radiance. We entered down three earthen steps leading to the concrete floor upon which the uncouth stone tombs stood, primitive in their lack of ornament. 'There is no need for the unearthly hush,' said the Count quietly. 'For us death is very much a part of everything. I am going to put this down here on Alecco's tomb to sustain his soul. Afterwards I shall offer you some more of it at home, my dear Zarian, to sustain your body. Is that not very Greek? We never move far in our metaphysical distinctions from the body itself. There is no incongruity in the idea that what fortifies our physical bowels, will also comfort Alecco's ghostly ones. Or do you think we are guilty of faulty dissociation?' Zarian and Theodore, more at home in the gloom now, potter the length of the vault. While Theodore characteristically examines the moss upon the walls and attempts to recall its medical name, Zarian concentrates upon a tomb in the corner which appears to be empty; the cracked stone lid lies beside it, as if it had fallen off in the struggles of the body to re-enter life. 'Ugly things, these tombs,' says the Count. 'Like the bunkers of a merchant ship. Ah! you are looking at the empty one. It used to belong to my Uncle John, who caused us a lot of trouble. He became a vampire, and so we had him moved to the

Landscape with Olive Trees

church behind the hill, where the ecclesiastical authorities could keep an eye on him. You did not know that the vampire exists?'

Walking back to the house across the green grass of the meadow, Theodore and the Count exchange reminiscences of vampiredom. The vampire is still believed in. It is known as a Vrikolax ($\beta\rho\nu\kappa o\lambda\alpha\xi$) and is the reward for an exceptionally evil life. In some cases vampires have been reported to have terrorized villages to such an extent that the Church has had to be called in to use its powers of exorcism. 'Uncle John,' says the Count, 'whom I remember as an old grey-whiskered ruffian in jack-boots, appears to have been an exceptionally wicked man. His reappearance was fully borne out by over two hundred witnesses, some of whose children had actually died. It was unpleasant, but they dug him up and put a stake into his heart in the traditional fashion. I felt that it was more politic to move him off the estate into the precincts of a church in order to avoid gossip.'

This theme, sufficiently exciting to wake Zarian from the abstraction into which his weekly Armenian article always throws him, also wakens Theodore in whom there lives a vague Edwardian desire to square applied science with comparative religion. The Count listens with exquisite politeness to a dissertation upon peasant lore. No one could guess that he has already heard it on several occasions. Throughout lunch, which we eat in the shade of the grape-arbour, Theodore unloads his evidence of pagan survivals in Greece—information which Zarian notes down excitedly on his cuff, on the tablecloth, in the battered notebook. Zarian's inveterate note-taking is a charming trait in his character—especially as he has never yet been known to succeed in reading his own notes afterwards, so cramped and illegible a hand has he. Theodore spends hours helping him to decode his own notes every Tuesday when the massive and erudite Armenian article must be begun.

During the afternoon, while the worthies of my Corcyrean pantheon are sleeping in shuttered rooms, I slip down to the house of the peasant family and borrow the Count's placid little mare, which will take me through the vineyards and woods to what is perhaps the loveliest beach in the world. Its name is Myrtiotissa. Lion-gold sand, of the consistency of tapioca, lies smoothly against the white limestone cliff, thrown up in roundels by the force of the sea, which breaks upon a narrow sand-bank some sixty yards clear of the shore. The rocks here are pitted and perforated into natural cisterns, sluggish with weed, and which the receding tide has left full of sea-water and winking fishes; water which the sun has heated to greater than the temperature of human blood. Lowering myself into these natural baths, holding softly to the ladder of many-coloured seaweed, I feel the play of the Ionian, rising and falling about an inch upon the back of my neck. It is like the heart-beat of the world itself. It is no longer a region or an ambience where the conscious or subconscious mind can play its incessant games with itself; but penetrating to a lower level still, the sun numbs the source of ideas itself, and expands slowly into the physical body, spreading along the nerves and bones a gathering darkness, a weight, a power. So that each individual finger-bone, each individual arm and leg, expand to the full measure of their own animal consciousness in this beneficent and dangerous sun-darkness. The scalp seems to put forth a drenched thatch of sea-weed to mingle with the weeds rising and falling around one's body. One is entangled and suffocated by this sense of physical merging into the elements around one. Blinded by this black sun-light, nothing remains of the known world, save the small sharp toothless kisses of fish on the hanging body—now no longer owned; a providential link with feeling, like the love of women, or the demands of the stomach, which tie one to the world of simple operations. One could die like this and wonder if it was death. The density, the weight and richness of a body without a mind or ghost to trouble it.

Here sometimes I come across Matthew, the lame dynamiter of fish, whose illegal operations in these bays have already cost him the sight of an eye and two fingers of his left hand. I help him to dive for those of his fish which for some mysterious reason sink instead of staying on the surface. On a fire of twigs in the evening we have often watched him grilling his fish with the absorbed air of a specialist, while Zarian stood by with the salt, and the Count with his little bottle of lemon-juice. Matthew chooses the afternoon for his fishing, as the noise of the detonations cannot then dissipate the heavy sleep of the policeman in the little guard house up the

Landscape with Olive Trees

hill. He is an admirable companion because he never speaks. Clad in patched clothes and the conventional woollen vest, he moves slowly along the rocky galleries above the sea, his prehensile black toes (now swollen and bloated with damp) gripping the rocky ledges. In his right hand he holds the home-made depth-charge, which is made from a cigarette tin and short length of fuse wire. I follow him at a safe range, to allow for any mechanical faults in this piece of machinery.

At about three o'clock he will invariably climb the cliff above the bay, to where the monastery stands in its dazzling white sunlight, and fall asleep in the shadow of the main gate with his silver catch lying in his old felt hat upon the grass.

Three hundred feet below, I cross the margin of scalding white sand, to the shadow of the great rock, and lie panting for a moment, too exhausted by running to move. Above me, leaking from the heart of the cliff, runs sweet water, down a shallow lip of maidenhair, into a sand-bowl; further to the left a mysterious spring rises in the very sand itself with little regular gushes, as if from some severed artery in the earth. At each soundless pulse a small cone of sand rises in the hollow and slowly spins back to the bottom. Clear and cold, the water plays with the regularity of a clock. It is the sweetest of the island waters, because it tastes of nothing but the warm afternoon, the breath of the cicadas, the idle winds crisping at little corners of the inert sea, which stretches away towards Africa, death-blue and timeless.

In this little bowl I wash the grapes I have brought with me. They are the little early grapes, delicately freckled green, and of a pouting teat-shape. The sun has penetrated their shallow skins and has confused the sweetness with its own warmth; it is like eating something alive.

Then after a rest another burst of running across the sand to where the cliff-path winds upwards, vertiginous and rocky, among the myrtle-groves. At the top of the cliffs, if you look back, you see the sea has become a deep throbbing emerald; the sand is freckled by long roaming silver lines across which an occasional lazy fish will move, indulgent of still water. In the shadows under the cliff a piercing nitric green. Far out across the water a brig moves southward into the sun; the noise of its engine is carried in the empty spaces of the air—a sound rubbed out as soon as registered, though nothing has breathed or stirred around one. A white butterfly wavers in across the blue spaces.

The mare snorts in the shadow of the peasant's house, glad to return. Half an hour later I am under the terrace upon which Zarian and Theodore sit, drinking tea from heavy Venetian-looking crockery, while the Count, an unfamiliar pipe alight in his mouth, sits and methodically cleans the coat of his favourite gun dog. It is inevitable that the discussion of this morning should be continuing. 'But, my dear Doctor,' the Count is saying placidly, 'I do not know how you can reconcile current religious beliefs without dragging in the ancient Pantheon. Our saints are not canonized and forgotten. They walk. The hagiography of St. Spiridion is still being written in those little two drachma books you buy outside the church. And then, the confusions. You have made a study of the folk-songs; have you found a very clear distinction made between the just and the unjust, or the idea of reward and punishment? No. The dead simply drink the waters of Lethe (της Λυσμονιάς τα νερά) and enter into a sort of mirage life, troubled by vague longings for fleshly joys—everything which we sum up in that most beautiful of Greek words Νοσταλγία. And then, of course, you have the Underworld, the Abode of the Dead. It is also known as Hades and as Tartarus, just to complete our confusion. And Charon, as you know, still exists, though he has altered his habits. Sometimes black snake, sometimes black swallow or eagle, he is also the Black Cavalier of our modern imaginations, dragging the souls of the dead behind him into the netherworld. And even he is credited in modern mythology with a wife. No. The only return for the dead seems to be for the unlucky or the evil; they become vampires and roam for a short while, until the Church catches up with them.'

Zarian is wearing his spectacles which means that he is paying extra close attention. Meanwhile Theodore nods his golden beard and, pouring out his tea into a saucer, blows upon it to cool it. The methodical fingers of the Count move through the shaggy coat of the animal, pulling off the fat white ticks, pursed with blood, one by one. 'And then the naiads', says the Count again, with his peculiar sweetness of voice, 'and the nereids that haunt our fountains and wells—what would we do without them? The shadow of the cypress which at noonday can drive a sleeper mad? The sea-maiden that winds her arms about those poor fishermen whom the full moon has overtaken on the strands?' Theodore is giving his famous grunt of disapproval which we have all learned to imitate. It is a kind of humming behind closed lips. 'You cannot, my dear Doctor,' continues the Count ruthlessly, 'make them compare with your scientific findings, yet we are glad to own them, even if they are lapses from the material attitude. They are part of the fantasy of this remarkable country and island, are they not?'

The dog whimpers softly as the strong antiseptic is applied to the little raw wounds left by the ticks; the Count's shapely hands cherish and soothe it. He looks up smiling, and watches Zarian disposing of a cake in short order. 'And think of the piercing lamentations of the professional mourners. I have made a collection of them—all spontaneous poetry, and some of the best known to the language. But there is no trace of the good-and-evil preoccupation. No, we Greeks are not religious, we are superstitious and anarchic. Even death is less important than politics. There is a kind of old Mother Hubbard who lives on the hill there; she is much in demand at funerals because of her poetic gift. Last year when Taki the fisherman died you should have heard her singing. It would have moved a stone.

> "My silver boy,
> My golden one,
> Softer the down on his face
> Than breast of the woodcock;
> Keener his mind than a snake striking.
> The silver person has left us.
> The golden man has gone."

'We carried him in his open box to the cemetery on the hill, and all the time this poetry was flowing out of Mother Hubbard in a continuous stream, keeping pace with her tears, for she really loved Taki.'

'Was the coffin open?' says Zarian.

'Yes. There again a point is proved.'

Landscape with Olive Trees

'Is that a religious custom of the island?'

'No. But under the Turks it was a law to prevent the smuggling of arms in coffins under the pretence of carrying corpses to the grave. In some places it has lingered on among the superstitious. So Taki's pale aquiline features were visible all the way as the ragged little procession wound up the hill. He looked as if he were about to smile. Of course no sooner was he dead and buried than Mother Hubbard, who was some vague relation, took out an injunction against his mother, to prevent her disposing of Taki's twenty olive-trees, which, she said, had been given to her as a gift. You see, there seemed to her no incongruity in making poetry for a dead man whom you love, and whose heirs you are trying to swindle. The case dragged on for months and I believe she lost it.'

As we talk we are watching out of the corner of our eyes the little party of sprayers which moves slowly down the rows of olive-trees. The foremost man holds the long canister with the tapering spout, through which he sprays a jet of arsenic and molasses, in a light cloud over each tree, to preserve the bloom against the ravages of its special pest. . . .

'It is fortunate', says the Count, 'to have a rich language. Look at my olive trees. How immeasurably they are enriched by the poetic symbolism which surrounds them—the platonic idea of the olives. The symbol for everything enriched by the domestic earth and private virtue. Then again, we use the word for those small dark moles which our women sometimes have on their faces or throats. And of course, being Greek, I find myself thinking at one and the same moment of all these facts, as well as the fact that the olive brings me in some eight hundred pounds a year on which to philosophize. Poetry and profit are not separated at all. For the Greek there is only the faintest dividing line.'

The evening light mellows very softly into its range of warm lemon tones, pressing among the close bunches of ripening grapes, and washing the tiles of the peasant houses in the valley. The turtle-doves croon softly in the arbours behind the orchard. The cicadas are dying out—station after station closing down. The two great plane-trees are already silent, and only in the meadow where the sun still plays do they keep up their singing. In the altering values of sound one becomes aware of the chink of teacups as the servant-girl clears away.

'The great god Pan', says the Count, reverting suddenly to his original theme, which has been running as an undercurrent in his thoughts all this time, 'was first announced as dead off Paxo, some miles south of us. This island must have been among the first to get the news. We have no records to tell us how the islanders received it. Yet in our modern pantheon we have a creature whose resemblance to Pan is not, I think, fortuitous. He is, as you know, called the kallikanzaros. He is the house-sprite, a little cloven-hooved satyr with pointed ears, who is responsible for turning milk sour, for leaving doors unlocked, and for causing mischief of every kind. He is sometimes placated by a saucer of milk left upon a window-sill, or a kolouri—one of those quoit-shaped peasant cakes. He also is dying out. But there is one story about him which you, my dear Zarian, will enjoy recording. It is said that on the ten days preceding Good Friday, all the kallikanzaroi in the Under-world are engaged simultaneously upon the task of sawing through the giant plane-tree whose trunk is supposed to hold up the world. Every year they almost succeed, except that the cry "Christ has arisen" saves us all, by restoring the tree and driving them up in a chattering throng into the real world—if I may call our world that. Perhaps you will be able to find classical origins for the story. I give it to you for what it is worth.'

Bats are now beginning their short strutting flights against the sky. In the east the colour is washing out of the world, leaving room for the great copper-coloured moon which will rise soon over Epirus. It is the magic hour between two unrealized states of being —the day-world expiring in its last hot tones of amber and lemon, and the night-world gathering with its ink-blue shadows and silver moonlight.

'Watch for her', says the Count, 'behind that mountain there.' The air tastes faintly of damp. 'She will be rising in a few moments.'

'I am thinking', says Zarian, 'how nothing is ever solved finally. In every age, from every angle, we are facing the same set of natural phenomena, moonlight, death, religion, laughter, fear. We make idolatrous attempts to enclose them in a conceptual frame. And all the time they change under our very noses.'

Landscape with Olive Trees

'To admit that,' says the Count oracularly, 'is to admit happiness—or peace of mind, if you like. Never to imagine that any of these generalizations we make about gods or men is valid, but to cherish them because they carry in them the fallibility of our own minds. You doctor, are scandalized when I suggest that *The Tempest* might be as good a guide to Corcyra as the official one. It is because the state of being which is recorded in the character of Prospero is something which the spiritually rich or the sufficiently unhappy can draw for themselves out of this clement landscape.'

'All this is metaphysics,' says Zarian a trifle unhappily.

'All speculation that goes at all deep becomes metaphysics by its very nature; we knock up against the invisible wall which bounds the prison of our knowledge. It is only when a man has been round that wall on his hands and knees, when he is certain that there is no way out, that he is driven upon himself for a solution.'

'Then for you, Count,' says Theodore, 'the hard and fast structure of the sciences yields nothing more than a set of comparative myths, some with and some without charm?'

'I would like to pose the problem from another angle. There is a morphology of forms in which our conceptual apparatus works, and there is a censor—which is our conditioned attitude. He is the person whom I would reject, because he prevents me choosing and arranging knowledge according to my sensibility. I will give you an example. I was once asked to write a short history of sixth-century Greek sculpture. My publisher refused the work because in it I had pointed out that sixth-century sculpture reaches its peak in Maillol, an artist of whom the man had not then heard. He informed me that I could not treat history in this manner. He informed me of the fact in the exact tone of voice used by my own censor when I first happened upon a Maillol statue, standing weighed down by its connections with the Mediterranean earth. Yet an instant's observation will show one that Maillol does not belong to us in space and time, but to them; I mean to the Greeks of the sixth century.'

At this point, according to time-honoured custom, we chant in unison: 'And if you don't believe me there is a Maillol in the

Landscape with Olive Trees

garden to *prove* it to you', at which the Count smiles his indulgent smile and nods twice. 'There is indeed,' he says.

The first bronze cutting-edge of the moon shows behind the mountain, travelling fast. 'Ah, there she is,' says Zarian.

'And here we are,' says the Count, unwilling to relinquish his subject, 'each of us collecting and arranging our common know-ledge according to the form dictated to him by his temperament. In all cases it will not be the whole picture, though it will be the whole picture for you. You, Doctor, will proceed under some title like *The Natural History, Geology, Botany and Comparative Ethnology of the Island of Corfu.* You will be published by a learned society in Vienna. Your work will contain no mention of the first edition of Petrarch in the Library, or of the beautiful mother of Gorgons in the Museum. As for you, Zarian, your articles when they are col-lected in a book will present a ferocious and lopsided account of an enchanted island which has seduced every historical figure of note from Nero to Napoleon. You will omit the fact that com-munications are bad and that all Greeks are liars, and that the fleas during the summer are intolerable. It will not be a true picture—but what a picture it will be. Hordes of earnest Armenians from New York will settle here to quote your poetry and prose to each other, and I will be able to charge two drachmae for sitting in the chair which you now occupy and which will certainly out-live you.'

'And I?' I say. 'What sort of picture will I present of Prospero's Island?'

'It is difficult to say,' says the Count. 'A portrait inexact in detail, containing bright splinters of landscape, written out roughly, as if to get rid of something which was troubling the optic nerves. You are the kind of person who would go away and be frightened to return in case you were disappointed; but you would send others and question them eagerly about it. You are to be forgiven really, because you have had the best of your youth in the island. And it is only very much later that one grows the courage to return. I noticed that you did not drink of Kardaki's well the other day. I particularly noticed.'

'I do not like being bound by charms,' I say.

At this point Theodore, who has been listening with some impatience to this dissertation upon character, suggests a stroll, and soon we are walking down the avenue of cypresses together, smelling the strong tobacco from the Count's pipe.

'Ah no, Doctor,' says the old man, as if continuing aloud an argument which has been going on quietly in his mind, 'thought must be free. Let us dispense with the formalist whose only idea is to eliminate the dissonant, the discrepant. Let us marry our ideas and not have them married for us by smaller people. Only in this way will our ideas produce children—for the children of ideas are actions. Dear me,' he adds, 'I am hardly in a position to moralize. I live here quietly without children, on money which my grandfather earned. It would be useless my justifying myself to an economist by explaining that I am exercising my sensibility through loving greatly and suffering greatly in all this quietness. Don't you think?'

Insensibly his footsteps have lead us across the green unkept lawns to where the nymph stands in her rotunda. Her loins fall away in their heavy inevitable lines to her shapely feet. The torso is heavy with its weight of lungs and bone. The breasts ride superbly, held by the invisible thongs of the pectorals.

'An old man's love,' says the Count. 'Look at her. There you have desire which is quite still, retained inside the mind as form and volume—like the grapes for lunch which were still warm and a little drowsy from the sun. It is the speechless potence of the old man, the most terrible kind of desire in stillness which this Mediterranean sculptor has impressed in the rock. Was he happy or unhappy, moral or amoral? He was outside the trap of the opposites. It was a mindless act of coition with the stone that made him describe her. Critics would be interested to know if it was his wife or his eldest daughter. Their speculations would lie right outside the realm in which this sixth-century Pomona stands. It is not desire as we know it—but an act of sex completed by looking at her. The weight of her. Feel how cold the stone arms are.'

The moon is up now among the trees, and the first screech of the owl rings out across the meadow.

'Ah! but I see they have lighted the candles and laid the table,' says the Count, suddenly conscious of the dew as he moves his toes in his battered felt slippers. 'And is it our function simply to stand about here making bad literature? Doctor, we are having brain cutlets in your honour this evening; and, my dear Zarian, a bottle of Mantinea red wine for you.'

Seated at the great table by the sedate light of his own candles, the Count turns to me and says: 'It is the pleasantest form of affection to be able to tease one's friends. You perhaps do not know the history of the Society of Ionian Studies and the brain cutlets?' At this Theodore shows the faintest signs of impatience, and remarking it, the Count pats him laughingly on the arm. 'The Doctor's well-known passion for brain cutlets is something of which you will have undoubtedly heard. Well, some years ago, he was asked to become President of a small informal society of local savants, who were bent on the pursuit of Ionian studies. They were a sombre and bearded collection—for the most part doctors and lawyers of the island: these being the two classes which have the least work to do. At this time our friend was pursuing some studies upon forms of idiocy at the local asylum; and he was particularly interested in the mental condition of an inmate called Giovannides, whose brain he had been coveting off and on for a number of years. In those days he used to speak about Giovannides' brain with ill-concealed cupidity, and explain what a splendid time he would have when the patient died. You see, he had been promised the brain for dissection. Now it so happened that this long-awaited event took place upon the very day when the inaugural lunch of the society was due to take place at the Doctor's house; Theodore was in a state of great excitement. He found himself unable to be patient, and spent the whole morning extracting the brain from its brain-case, remembering all the time that he must get home and prepare his speech for the Society. By midday he had succeeded in removing the brain, and, having wrapped it carefully in greaseproof paper, he had managed to reach home with it held in his arms like a precious treasure. On entering the house he realized that the day was exceptionally warm, so he entered the kitchen, where he popped the lunatic's brain in the ice-box, and retired to his study to prepare his speech. All went well. The guests arrived and were seated at table. The speech was delivered and met with restrained applause. And a steaming dish of the Doctor's favourite brain-cutlets appeared,

which was greeted with delighted exclamations. As the guests were
helping themselves the telephone in the corner of the room rang.
It was Theodore's wife, who had rung up to apologize for having
been unable to provide him with his favourite dish for lunch.
There was, she said, no brain to be bought anywhere in town. An
involuntary cry burst from Theodore's lips. To do him justice, it
was not really of his guests that he was thinking so much as of his
brain. With a muffled cry of "Giovannides' brain" he sprang to
the kitchen and opened the ice-box. The brain had gone. Speechless with anxiety the good doctor returned to the banqueting-room
and found that his guests were all looking either uneasy or down-
right ill. Where a lesser man would have carried it off without
telling them anything definite, and where a greater would have
wrung his hands for science, Theodore simply stood, trembling
from head to foot and pointing at the dish of excellent brain-
cutlets and repeating: "I get a brain and *this* is what you do. I
get a brain and *this* is what you do." By this time the truth had
dawned upon the Ionian Society; their dissolution was so sudden
as to be amazing. The maid threw her apron over her head and
burst into sobs. The inaugural lunch was a failure. But that was
not the unkindest thing of all. The brain of the lunatic was at this
moment safely upon Theodore's desk, in the study; the cook, who
was devoted to Theodore, had spent the whole morning searching
for brain, and had found some in the nick of time. The cutlets
served to the Society were perfectly genuine brain cutlets. But do
you think he has ever managed to persuade anyone of the truth
of this? No. The Society is now referred to as the Brainfever
Society, and its members are all supposed to be suffering from
aberrations brought on by this meal.'

This anecdote, which we have heard perhaps a dozen times,
always sinks Theodore into a profound gloom; for Zarian laughs
so immoderately that he spills his wine, and has a fit of coughing
until he almost rolls under the table. This is the Count's cue, and
turning to him on the backwash of his laughter he says: 'But perhaps Zarian will permit me to tell you the story of his explorations
into Greek wines.' At this, it is Zarian's turn to look uncomfortable, while Theodore's face is lit by a shy smile. 'You will have
noticed,' says the Count, 'that Zarian champions everything

Landscape with Olive Trees

Greek except the wines. It is true they are not very good, but you would expect a few romantic notes to be blown from time to time on his trumpet. No, I might go so far as to say that he is definitely against Greek wine, and I often wonder whether the little incident of the Mantinea 1936 had anything to do with it. May I repeat the story in my own way?' he asks Zarian with elaborate courtesy. The latter runs his fingers through his mane of silver hair, braces his shoulders as one about to bear a burden, and humbly nods. It is charming to watch him ill-at-ease, picking at the tablecloth, searching for non-existent matches in the pockets of his waistcoat, or shaking his finger in his ear with an expression of simulated pain. The Count sips his wine twice, fills my glass, and continues.

'Late one night last year I received a telephone call. The voice was so full of suppressed excitement that I had difficulty in recognizing it as that of Zarian. He had, he said, something of the utmost importance to tell me. The revelation was too secret to be mentioned on the phone, but I gathered that something very frightful or very wonderful had happened to him. At that time I was in the town house, so I agreed to walk across the Esplanade and see my friend. To be frank, I thought he had simply written a poem. As we all know, when Zarian writes one of his rare poems, he telephones to all his friends and asks them to come round and have it read to them. It was not a poem or an accident. When I climbed those tottering stairs to the top floor of the St. George Hotel I found my friend sitting in a room at a table, staring with considerable rigidity at an open bottle of wine. A single candle guttered beside it on the table Catching sight of me, he beckoned me speechlessly into the room and into a chair opposite. For a moment he said nothing but continued to stare at the bottle of wine. Then at last he spoke in accents positively strangled by excitement. "My dear Count," he said, "I have at last discovered a Greek wine comparable to anything grown in France." He tiptoed to a cupboard and brought me a glass which he filled very gingerly, holding his breath as he did so. I sipped it. It was a very fine Beaune, ringing on the palate like a note of music. The bottle said MANTINEA 1936, and I knew that Mantinea was an ordinary table wine. I congratulated him and drank some more. Zarian was by this time walking up and down in a state of considerable excitement. "A wine for the Gods," he kept repeating. I noticed that he was in his socks. His feet, he said, hurt him. He had been walking round the town since four in the afternoon buying up all the wine of this name and date he could find. My impulse there and then was to warn him against undue optimism, but his pleasure was so warming a sight that I let him ramble on. Finally he lead the way into his wife's bedroom, holding the candle high, in order to let me see the seventy or eighty bottles of the wine lying snugly upon the bed. I remember that he held his finger over his lips and spoke in whispers, for all the world as if we were in danger of waking the bottles up. It took us an hour to finish the bottle with our conversation growing more and more exalted. Zarian felt that the last link to bind him to Corcyra had been forged; always fussy about wine, he had been unable to get used to the heavy sweet products of Greece. When we had disposed of the first bottle his magnanimity lead him to tiptoe into the bedroom and come back with another. He opened it with a flourish, poured some out, and sipped. An expression of disgust came over his face. He held the wine for a moment only in his mouth before bounding to the window and spitting it out. It was obviously a faulty bottle. With a dawning look of alarm on his face he retired and fetched two more bottles. They were both full of superior vinegar. He opened a dozen. They were all the same. I left him that evening surrounded by opened bottles of Mantinea, which he was pouring away down the kitchen sink. The glorious Beaune was never repeated. And now when I offer him a glass of Mantinea—which is after all not a very bad wine as wines go—you observe the face he makes.'

Zarian, to whom the subject of wine is sacred, does not find the story in very good taste, one can see. Yet he suffers it admirably; and later upon the dazzling white terrace, sipping his cognac, he confesses that he is developing a taste for retzina. 'It is not to be drunk alone, but with meat and vegetables cooked in the peasant manner. Lamb with onions, egg-plant, potatoes, and that red sauce which you all know. Then it tastes like a divine turpentine.'

'But speaking of intoxicating drinks,' says Theodore, 'I wonder, Count, if you have remarked that arbutus berries are among the things which can also intoxicate. During the campaigns of Macedonia during the last war I noticed that on several occasions

Landscape with Olive Trees

battalions of our troops became quite drunk through eating the berries of the shrub. In some cases their wits seemed turned by the habit. I often wonder whether in Xenophon the mysterious outbreak of madness among the troops could have come from the same cause.'

It is ten o'clock and the moonlight is dazzling. Across the valley I can see the shallow glare of Spiro's headlamps flash as he brings N. to me. We are off to explore the caves near Paleocastrizza and spend the night in the small hotel there. The demented honking with which Spiro always announces his approach sounds sweet and muffled across the silver trees.

Loath to disrupt the speculative calm of my three philosophers I get up and say good-bye. The Count insists on accompanying me the length of the terrace to send a message to N. Faint interior preoccupations stir behind his composed features. 'And you are coming for the vintage don't forget,' he says. 'Bring her with you. It is a time for women.' Then he adds almost apologetically, 'We do not consider them enough perhaps.' And I know all at once that his thoughts have turned to the Roman nymph standing in the rotunda with the leaves turning over around her feet. I would like to say something that was not redundant or out of place but can find no words. The very fabric of this candid and beautiful landscape forbids it. I shake his hand and walk down the long avenue to the gates where the great car stands panting with Spiro jovial behind the wheel.

The western waters of Paleocastrizza will be icy cold to-night; and under the castle of St. Angelo the silver race will be combing out its long strands. Soon there is to be a war.

7.4.38

Coming over the crest of the hill behind Kastellani we see that a dance is in progress. From the grassy glades below, the shadow of the olive-trees is broken by clouds of dust, and the afternoon silence by the terrific giggling of donkeys—like pantomime comedians. Smoke from the fires, upon which whole kids are turning upon spits, rises lazily. Through the hum of human voices one can hear the scratch and squeak of the violin and guitars, and the hollow beat of the drum, resonant and vulgar as a full stomach struck with the palm of the hand. 'Ah look,' says N. 'Just look at the dancers.'

A multi-coloured circle of flowing head-dresses and skirts moves slowly about the axis of the musicians, reversing and advancing with slow rhythmic measures. In the centre of the circle, moved by the current, but free, the young men dance, each improvising his variations upon the theme, hand on hip, head thrown back, face devout and abstract. In the luminous shadows among the trees the crowds are laughing and chattering, the pedlars of ikons, talismans, or bread and sweets, resting for a while upon the boles of the olives in expressive poses. Whiffs of roasting lamb and wine come across the clearing where the old men and women are sitting in groups upon the grass like birds, eating and drinking. Father Nicholas is there in his blue trousers watching his younger son dancing, all dressed in white, with a fine new straw hat upon his square head. Sandos and his daughter are sitting under an olive-tree. Socrates and Demosthenes are eating themselves silly by the turning lambs. Several of the girls from our northern village are in the outer circle; one recognizes them by the sobriety of their costume—black clothes with white head-dress. Here districts still keep their distinctions of head-dress; and in Corfu the women of Gastouri are justly renowned as the most beautiful and the most colourful. Here in the circle of dancers you can see the famous full pleated skirt of shot silk and the old-fashioned bodice, under a bolero heavy with gold stitching—the crust of embroidery. Gold drops dangle at the ear, while the coiffure is a marvellous erection —built up towards the back of the head in tiers, worked over little cloth pads, and tied with red ribbon. A lace-edged handkerchief turned back from the crown, frames the handsome olive face.

'Ah,' says Theodore with pleasure, 'it is a star-dance, called the Corcyrean Dance. As you may know I have theories about the origin of these dances, some of which are very ancient.'

The multi-coloured wheel spins and reverses, spins and reverses, while the lone-moving satellites plot out their intricate measures. The fiddlers have their heads together in a conspiracy of rhythm. The two violins drizzle steadily. The son of Father Nicholas throws his head back from time to time and gives a short excited cry of pleasure as his deft feet in their heavy boots glide and spin upon

Landscape with Olive Trees

the green turf, now being beaten to dust by the moving feet of the women. Strange associations come to mind. The wheel of the heavens. The repeating tread of the women, as if caught in the labyrinth of the rhythm, the measure repeating itself, multiplied only by the free improvisations of the men. The mating dance of birds.

'All the circular ones I call star dances,' says Theodore. 'I read somewhere that dancing originated in a desire to imitate the movement of celestial bodies—the early clock as it were.'

The boy in white is dancing now with the faultless inevitability of someone for whom nothing else exists. His head is thrown back and his sharp nostrils dilated. He has thrown his hat out of the circle, to roll unerringly at Father Nicholas's feet under the olives. His brown hair rises and falls on his head. One hand is at his hip, upon the red sash he is wearing; the other is posed at full length like that of a conductor, expressing every subtlety of gesture and balance. He is dancing before the girl in yellow and blue—a swarthy Gastouri beauty—with heavy limbs. Her face is flushed as he reaches out the handkerchief for her to touch. The women, linked together, struggle and cry like gulls. Nearer he dances and nearer. He does not look at her but you feel at once a correspondence, a power, flowing between them. For a moment her face looks panic-stricken and dazed; and then she reaches out her strong brown paw and takes the hem of the handkerchief between her fingers. The music rolls over them. They rotate, buried in the rhythms, latched together by this fateful contact, revolving together in the communion of sound and action.

Father Nicholas has been watching them with a strange mixture of pride and resentment in his face. Of course as a northerner he should not be making advances to a Gastouri girl. Seeing us, however, his smiles reappear and he hobbles across to greet us as quickly as his rheumatism allows. When he speaks I observe that his breath is heavy with wine. 'The young are only young once,' he tells us several times in a voice deepened an octave by red wine. Kastellani is his favourite brew. 'When they dance all the sins of the world dance with them. When I was young. . . .' But the uproar is too great for him to be allowed to reminisce. We are presented in quick succession to the mayor, two policemen, and

Landscape with Olive Trees

three monks (who timidly hide their glasses of wine behind a tree before coming across to shake hands). N. begins making her slow painful notes for paintings—a donkey with panniers, an old woman, a policeman lying asleep under a tree with his tunic unbuttoned, a man making a drunken political speech which is completely inaudible above the music.

Zarian sits down upon the earth ledge outside a cottage to mop his silver head. Through the open door one can see one of those strange interiors: a huge carved bed which takes up nearly the whole room, with the ikons of the saints at its head, and on the nail above it the green marriage wreath. 'The Corfiots expend all their decorative talent upon their beds,' says Zarian cynically; 'shall I tell you why? It is not because the bed is the place where they get most pleasure out of life—but because it is the only article in the house which by law is not seizable for debt.'

The dance has changed now to a slower and more stately tempo. The circle begins to wheel. The circle of chance. The wheel of fate. The boy in white is still dancing before the Gastouri girl. She is smiling in a silly tranced way, like a hypnotized bird, as she clutches the handkerchief.

'Making love, marrying, having children and dying,' says Zarian again, addressing nobody but himself. 'Is there no escape from the circle at all?'

Nicholas is upon us with drinks now as the twilight sets in. A priest is examining my sandals with admiration. A rather good-looking villager is making over-friendly remarks to N. who is replying in her bad Greek as best she can.

Theodore, to everyone's surprise, has taken off his coat, and clad in braces and black boots has entered the circle to dance. A cheer goes up. His blond beard flashes in the waning sunlight. Hand on hip he does a few hesitating measures, and then suddenly transfixed by the rhythm begins to dance very well. The women are enchanted by this blond bearded man. 'An Englishman,' they cry. 'No. No,' yells Father Nicholas hoarsely from under the trees. 'A Greek by God. A Greek from Thessaly.' Subdued applause. Head cocked to the music Theodore dances, looking more than ever like an Ionian faun. 'But he is like an Englishman,' cry the women. The voices of men under the trees chorus back: 'No. He is a Greek

Landscape with Olive Trees

in spite of the beard.' Father Nicholas gives the Abbot of Myrtiotissa a stately dig in the ribs. 'Go on and dance, good father,' he
says, 'you have a beard too. Dance.' The Abbot giggles coyly. He
is rather afraid of the fierce old man. 'Dance,' yells Nicholas with
more abandon. 'All you priests ought to dance.' And he gives him
a resounding smack upon the back and spills his wine. A policeman absently fires his pistol in the air for the sheer fun of it. A
donkey breaks loose and ambles through the crowd with two small
shrieking children in the panniers on its back. One of the monks
mounts it and drives it back to the trees with shrill cries. A fresh
round of wine appears from nowhere and gruff healths ring out,
mingled with belches.

Theodore reappears mildly and says that it is time to start. We
have a long walk to make yet before we reach the town. 'Doctor,
that was well done,' cries Father Nicholas in ringing tones. Theodore smartly sidesteps to avoid the approbation of Father Nicholas's palm which at this stage in the feast falls heavily on friend and
enemy alike. 'With dancing like that you should win many beautiful women.' Saying good-bye, we take the road and climb slowly
to the next hillock, from which the dance seems remote and
mystical—like a coloured heart beating there under the trees. At
this range the violins and guitars are inaudible. Only the little
bump of the drum still sounds on in our ears.

Turning towards the east we walk silently down the scented
road in the deep dust. 'I do not think, Doctor,' says Zarian, 'that
the circular dances have anything to do with the stars. I am sure
this kind of dancing originated out of some purely practical impulse or occupation. Now I suggest that the circular dances are
really symbolic representations of the threshing floor, that they are
grain dances. Again, in the dance known as the Trata you can see
that it is based upon the fishermen pulling at a net.'

Theodore is not disposed to quarrel about this interpretation.
We walk down the long winding road into the valley in silence.
At a corner we come upon a pedlar asleep in the ditch with his hat
over his face. Beside him lies a pack full of trinkets; blue beads
against the evil eye, amulets, and tracts about the works of the
Saint. He snores wonderfully in the deep grass, with one arm
thrown in abandon over his face and the other stretched out to its

full length. 'Ah, sweet content,' says Zarian. 'We always miss you. We think too much. What are the odds on all this speculation we indulge in if for once we cannot go to a dance, drink a glass of wine, and fall asleep in the ditch like a Greek god on holiday?'

'Or wake in the morning with lice in our hair and a hangover,' says Theodore severely.

'It will be wonderful to have a bath,' says N.

'And dinner. And then to walk across to the open-air cinema where we shall see *The Sign of the Cross*—this ancient film about the life of Christ, which has caused such a stir in the island. The ecclesiastical authorities are trying to have it banned.'

'It is not so much the film,' says Theodore, 'as the fact that the Corfu daily newspaper carried on its news-page the headline: CHRIST TO APPEAR IN CORFU. The general public grew quite alarmed by the idea.'

The moon is rising.

8.8.38

Bocklin has walked over the hills from Metsovo, and arrived in the island. In our Paris days he was a seedy blond youth, so that we hardly recognize the tough-looking specimen of the new Germany who stands on our doorstep. He has with him a number of his own photographs and drawings which are full of life and sensibility. We spend the week-end together at the Count's country house, where he gets a chance to unload his treasury of demotic songs and fables. He speaks Greek perfectly. Zarian and Theodore are captivated by his manners and his gaiety, and the way he sings to the guitar.

In the morning while the Count and I are looking for swallows' nests under the eaves we enter his room and see a bundle of accurate architectural drawings of the main harbour and fortress.

9.8.38

Riding south from Paleocastrizza in a fair wind we come to Ermones beach just before dawn; and swimming ashore in the grey half light we build in gleaming sand the figure of a gigantic recumbent Aphrodite. N. and Veronica model the face while Dorothy and I shape the vast thighs. We give her a crown of pebbles for pearls and a belt made from withes of sapling, like snakes. She lies staring at the lightening sky, her mouth open in an agonizing shriek, being born. While the sea creeps up and gnaws her long rigid fingers.

By first sunlight we are away again, wondering what the wide-eyed fisher-boys will make of this great relief in sand. Aphrodite rising from the foam.　*

15.8.38

Theodore says that in the mountains, where shepherds must pasture their flocks half the year round in the fastnesses far from any village, it is customary to have a ewe instead of a wife. Far from betraying any unusual sensitivity to a practice so well known, each shepherd has his own favourite ewe, which he tricks out with bells and tassels according to his fancy. This ewe is known as the favourite one. The Greek word is *Λαγιαρνὶ*.

He records a conversation with one of the shepherds in Epirus which carries the authentic Holborn Empire note of cynicism. 'What point is there', asked Theodore in his academic manner, 'in having this ridiculous practice?' (He was referring to the trinkets which adorned one of the chosen ewes.)

The shepherd thought for a moment and then replied, as one who offers an opinion verified by long personal experience: 'From every point of view they are superior to our wives. But above all they do not talk.'

VII

The Vintage Time

20.9.38

Riding southward in the spluttering bus from Kouloura to
Ypso at the end of a bright September you can feel the
altered accent in things—for the vintage is beginning.
Everywhere the turtle-doves are calling in the arbours
and orchards; and washed by the brilliant sunlight the whole
coast glitters and expands under the swinging blows of the waves.
The bay is alive with sails glowing in their many colours, and the
atmosphere is so clear that one can see, miles away, the distinct
figures of friends holding sails and tillers; my brother's boat *Dugong*
lies just off Agni, heading for the house. I can see his characteristic
pose, legs stretched out, head on one side and eyes closed against
the smoke of his cigarette. He has stowed his guns in their leather
cases under the half-decking where the faithful Spiro sits scanning
the horizon for something to shoot at. *Dugong* slaps and yaws as she
meets the small race of water thrown back, yellow and curdled,
from the Butrinto Estuary. He will be sorry to miss us on his way
up to the northern lake Antiniotissa ('Enemy of youth') where he is
after quail and woodcock.

As we move slowly down from the dead lands the road becomes
more and more precipitous, and the green valley comes up at us in
a trembling wave of fronds and branches. We roar through several
small hamlets, scattering smoke and stones. A woman stands
frowsily at her door and empties coffee grounds upon the stones.
Two children sit under a bench playing with a tortoise. A policeman shouts something unintelligible. The bus is crammed with
peasants going to market, and the air in it smells almost inflam-
mable with garlic and exhaust fumes. Father Nicholas and his son
sit just behind us. He has finally conquered his prejudice against
southern women, and they are on their way to try and arrange a
match with the Gastouri girl whom we had seen at the Kastellani

120

The Vintage Time

dance. Father Nicholas is in great voice and keeps the whole bus in a roar of laughter. Our feet rest upon a fluttering floor of chickens, all tied by the legs in bunches, like vegetables. His son looks rather ashamed of himself. It is not altogether restful, this journey. At each of Father Nicholas's jests the driver lets off a peal of laughter in a high piping voice and, letting go his hold upon the wheel, hugs himself with extravagant joy. At these moments the bus shows signs of wanting to mount the stone parapet of the road and fly down into the valley. This tendency is corrected at the last moment, when all except the hardiest travellers have commended themselves to St. Spiridion and flung one arm across their eyes. With prodigious roaring and scraping of brakes we rattle down the mountain like some iron cockroach, and draw up at last in clouds of dust, before the little tavern at the crossroads where Spiro had already parked his great Dodge under the olives, and is busy arguing about the price of wine with the innkeeper.

We sit for a while over a glass of wine with him. He gives us the gossip of the town in his wonderful Brooklyn argot—strange fragments of words with whole syllables discarded from them when they are beyond his pronunciation. Spiro's noble stomach reposes comfortably on his knees. His forearms are covered in a black pelt of hair. He is sweating easily and comfortably from every pore. In the dark shadow thrown by the trees, with the red reflections of the tablecloth playing about his dark, good-natured face, he reminds me of nothing so much as a great drop of olive oil. He informs us, with self-importance mixed with a certain shame, that a fire broke out the previous afternoon at a garage. As one of the firemen he had had his first practical experience of fire-fighting. On the whole the affair had been rather a scandal. The brigade had arrived in good time, clinging importantly to the new fire-engine which the Government had provided, each in his gleaming helmet. Spiro himself had arrived, but riding majestically in his own car, with his helmet on. The garage was well alight. The balconies of the surrounding houses were thronged with sightseers, waiting to see the recently formed Fire Brigade prove itself in its first baptism of fire. All went well. While the hose was being uncoiled, the Chief of Police made a short but incisive speech exhorting everyone to stay calm and not to give way to panic. The fire hydrant was unlocked and everything placed in position to extinguish the blaze. At this point, however, a disgraceful argument broke out as to who was going to hold the nozzle of the hose. Words became gestures. Gestures became acts. A push here, a scuffle there, and riot had broken out. A struggling mass of firemen began to fight for possession of the nozzle. At this point the hose bulged and began to emit a creditable jet of water, and what was to be a baptism of fire became a baptism of water for the onlookers. A slowly rotating fountain of water moved across the square. The Minister for the Interior, who had been standing innocently on his balcony in heliotrope pyjamas, was all but swept into the street by the force of the jet. Women screamed. The long-averted panic against which the Chief of Police had warned them broke out. The affair ended with a baton charge and a number of arrests. The garage was left to burn itself out. The engine was driven home in disgrace by a civilian. And Spiro tendered his resignation.

Driving easily across the low hills where the vineyards have already taken on their ochre tones, he seems a little hurt that we find the story funny. 'It's not a good thing', he tells N. repeatedly, 'for the nation when the bastards do that.'

We sweep up the long drive and round to the side of the house. The Count is sitting at the edge of the orchard, under a tree, reading with his dogs beside him. He is clad in pyjamas and a straw hat. He waves his hand and signals us to cross the sunlight-dappled walks.

'Ah! you will forgive my pyjamas,' he says. 'The others have not arrived yet. I am half drunk just reading through Mazziari's description of the grapes. Come, let us take our pick.'

The vineyards are already beginning to look gutted and burnt out with shrivelling leaves. The Count walks ahead with us stopping here and there in all the profusion to clip a bunch of grapes with his scissors, which he carries tied round his waist on a piece of string. 'Ah, my dear, where have you ever seen such plenty?' he says. Indeed the variety is astonishing. 'We will ignore these plump ones with the thick skins. But try these violet coloured ones. You may find them too sweet. We have had three days' torture preparing for the gathering. So many extra mouths to feed. Plasterers, treaders, and whatnot hanging about the house.' The great

The Vintage Time

doors of the magazine are ajar. The huge vats and butts have been dragged out into the meadow for caulking and patching. Under a tree a small army of men is at work upon them. Some have been turned upon logs, and are being filled with gravel and water, before being rolled. Others are being mended and scoured. 'The big one in the corner,' says the Count, 'she is the one you have to thank for the crimson robola wine which you think so good—and which even Zarian likes.'

The shadow of the cottage-pergolas seems rich with the scent of grapes—of blunt sweet muscatel and lisabetta. Ourania cuts down heavy clumps of them for the table, holding them in her brown arms and smiling. They are covered in a rich misty bloom still.

Meanwhile across the orchard the Count is in full voice: 'The little amber ones and those which look ice-green and closely packed—they have done very well this year. Farther on we shall see the *rhoditi*. They run blood-red when the sun shines through them; coral rather, like the lobe of an ear. Dear me, we shall all have indigestion. Ah! Here comes the Doctor and Zarian—beyond the olive-trees there. And his wife. Zarian looks extremely puffed as usual. And Nimiec.'

By lunch-time the rest of the guests have arrived, and are seated at tables laid under the arbour which bounds the last terrace. A tremendous meal has been prepared, and three of the prettiest village girls are there to serve it. Zarian openly bemoans having brought his pleasant American wife with him. 'Where do you keep these beauties?' he asks. 'They are never here when we come alone.'

'They would distract us perhaps,' says the Count seriously. The crimson *robola* is passed round. Each pours a drop upon the ground before drinking—the peasant libation. The grounds are swarming with workmen to prepare for to-morrow's picking.

'This year we are going to begin on the hill there. It should be specially good, this year's *robola*. I feel it in my bones. We shall call it, I think, Prospero's Wine. What do you say?'

The valley curves away below the arbour with its delicately curved panels of landscape. From the orchard a guitar strikes up, and after a few moments' hesitation the sound of voices—the men's deep and rough, the women's high and shrill as herring-gulls'. The

The Vintage Time

gatherers have arrived in the hope of an extra day's work. The faint crack of guns sounds in the valley. A puff of smoke here and there marks a sportsman with a muzzle-loader shooting doves. The conversation wells up in waves—overstepping the boundaries of language. The vintage holiday has begun.

Lunch prolonged unconscionably becomes tea. Some of us wander away to bathe or sleep out the long hot afternoon. By nightfall the gang of workmen have done their job, and the vine-vats are ready. They sit upon doorsteps or on the grass among the olive-trees, eating their frugal meal of bread and fruit. But wine there is in plenty for them.

At the end of the terrace Zarian lies majestically sleeping in a hammock, while his wife pauses from her reading at intervals to brush a fly off his face. Theodore and Nimiec have disappeared on a journey of exploration with N.

The Count is pottering round the magazine in his pyjamas giving orders in a peremptory voice to his overseers. 'To-morrow we shall start on the *robola* vat,' he says, and gives orders for it to be moved out of the shadow into the angle of the wall where the sunlight strikes. 'Niko is going to come and do the treading. I can always trust him.' Niko is a slim young man, dressed in a dark suit, who holds his hat modestly in his hand as he hears the Count speak. 'If we put all the women on to the vineyard at once we should have the first vat gathered by sundown to-morrow. Niko can begin at dusk.' His face is radiant and empty of preoccupation. Meanwhile the cellars must be tidied, the magazines dusted and all vanishable goods removed beyond the reach of the pickers' temptation. Ourania is filling the bowls with flowers—autumn crocus and cyclamen from the walls of the vineyards. Donkeys unload mounds of red tomatoes at the outhouse and everywhere the brisk sound of bargaining goes on. Caroline is playing patience upon the balcony, stopping from time to time to pop a grape into her mouth. 'We cannot complain,' says the Count. 'It will be a lovely vintage. We can start Niko off to-morrow. We might bathe to-night. We can use the car. I see that Spiro has stayed on with us. It's bad for trade but he can't bear to miss a party.'

The sound of singing is beaten out thin upon the late afternoon air. I can hear Spiro's bass notes sounding like the eructations of

The Vintage Time

a giant. The Count sits for a while on the garden wall with one slipper off and lights a cigarette. 'And perhaps we shall have an engagement or something to remind us that we are getting old men.' Caroline pretends she does not hear.

Bocklin has brought his flute. Its quaint twirls and flourishes sound unearthly on the empty lawns where the nymph stands. The Count walks slowly down the garden path. 'There is going to be a war, of course. But on days like this one feels that it will go on for ever—I mean this lovely lambent weather: no sense of time, except that the fruit upon our tables changes. By the way, figs are in. Let us hope they will outlive your foreign policy, my dear boy. I see you have been reading Mackenzie. It will be just the same. The Royalists will let us down all the way along. Don't you see that Nimiec and Caroline are falling in love with each other? There is that subtle unspoken polarity of feeling you can see when they are together. They both know it will happen. They both know that the other knows. They both avoid each other's company. And yet the invisible cobweb is drawing tighter. That is happiness—the certainty and inevitability of an attraction like that. It remains for the lock to turn on the event and already it is spoiled. They have had a hundred opportunities to confess themselves—and there he is walking round with the Doctor, holding his test-tubes, while she sits and plays patience and imagines that she does not want him to come and find her there. You know, there is no philosophic compensation for growing beyond the reach of love—that is the one wall one never breaks through. To think that *that* will never happen again. That *that* moment, the germinating half-second during which you recognize your completement in someone else, will never happen again. . . . Any of the peasant girls would supply the physical simulacrum of the event. Ah, but the thing itself is gone. Let us have a glass of wine, shall we? It's thirsty work talking like a Norman Douglas character. Caroline, have a glass of wine with us and let me tell your fortune.'

Just after dawn the cries of the pickers wake us. The grass is still heavy with dew and the sun not yet above the trees. A long line of coloured women are setting forth for the vineyard with their

The Vintage Time

baskets. Mark and Peter are the overseers, and they follow with lordly strides behind them smoking and talking, proud in their blue smocks and straw hats. Spiro follows with the brindled puppy. As we watch the procession the window below us opens and the Count puts his head out to cheer them with some parting pleasantry. The early breakfast daunts everyone but Zarian, who has eaten himself into a state of feverish indigestion and cannot sleep. Spiro sits on the terrace, cap in hand, and prophesies a sunny day in the voice of such heartiness that Zarian becomes all at once quite peevish. The Count, having reassured himself that the pickers have set out to gather the favourite *robola* vineyard, sleeps on for a couple of hours.

By mid-morning we are all up on the hillock overlooking the vineyard, surrounding our pyjama'd host like staff officers watching a battle. On the brilliant dappled sunlight of the slopes below the women have put on their wimples and are moving with swift grace from shrub to shrub, cutting the long branches with their sickle knives—branches of crimson *robola* which droop in their baskets with the weight of human limbs.

In the shade of an olive cloths have been spread, and here the women converge, each with her blooming basket load. Two donkeys with panniers stand by apathetically, flicking flies with their tails. Everything goes with a terrific pace for this the first day of picking and the Count himself is looking on.

Presently, when the Count has been reassured as to the picking, we retire to the arbours by the house to drink coffee and pass the long morning in idle talk. Bocklin plays his flute. And gradually, by journeys, the donkeys bring in the fruit which is emptied into the great wooden vat under the careful eyes of Niko himself. The Count cannot sit still until he has supervised everything himself, and seen everything with his own eyes. 'Niko is a wonderful boy,' he says. 'Don't think that any oaf can tread wine. No, he is pure as island water. Don't imagine that the wine-treader doesn't transform the wine with his feet—that there isn't a communication I mean between his style and technique and state of soul and the response of the fruit. It's an aesthetic performance. No, Doctor. It is no use you smiling in that ironical scientific manner. We could easily use a machine-treader and you would soon see what sort of

The Vintage Time

wine my *robola* had become. Niko treads a part of himself into the vat. He is an angel on earth. Ah! dear me. How over-exotic one sounds when one translates from Greek to English.'

By four o'clock the vat is heaped full and from the sheer black weight of the fruit the must has begun to force the crude spigot. The Count is extremely excited, for it is the moment to begin the treading. Niko has been standing in the trough by the well, washing himself in the icy water. Now he advances to the vat, clad only in a white shirt which is knotted at the thighs. His pale face looks remote and far-away as he hoists himself up. His white feet dangle for a second in the sunlight and vanish. The Count is hoarse with emotion. 'You remember everything now,' he says nervously. 'The old way—as you have done it always.' Niko does not answer. He smiles, as if at some remembered joke, and nods. Gently moving his feet he begins by treading a small hole to stand in and begins to work into it the grapes piled above the rim.

The spigot is now uncorked and the must begins to come out in an opaque crimson spurt. This beautiful colour stains the trough, lacquers the tin measure, and stabs the shadows of the magazine with splashes of red. Keeping the same tireless pace Niko labours deeper and ever deeper into the great vat until by the latest dusk his white face has quite vanished into the depths and only his two crimson grape-splashed hands can be seen holding the edges of the vat. He perches himself up every now and again and rests, hanging his head like a bird. He has become almost intoxicated himself by the fumes of the must, and by the long six-hour routine of his treading—which ends at ten o'clock. His face looks pale and sleepy in the red light of the lanterns. Mark encourages him with gruff pleasantries as he measures the must back into the vat. Since the wine is red the skins and stalks are left in. Now the huge wooden lid, weighted with stones, is floated upon the top, and by to-morrow morning all the leavings will have risen up under it into a scarlet froth of crust, from under which the liquid will be crackling with fermentation. For ten days now the fermentation will go on, sending its acid smell on the gusts of wind from the meadow, into the bedrooms of the great house.

Now that the *robola* is safely on the way, the Count can turn his attention to the kitchens with their gleaming copper ware and dungeon-like ovens. Here he busies himself with Caroline and Mrs. Zarian in the manufacture of *mustalevria*—that delicious Ionian sweet or jelly which is made by boiling fresh must to half its bulk with semolina and a little spice. The paste is left to cool on plates and stuck with almonds; and the whole either eaten fresh or cut up in slices and put away in the great store cupboard.

Sykopita, Zarian's favourite fig cake, will come later when the autumn figs are literally bursting open with their own ripeness. But for the time being there are conserves of all kinds to be made— orange-flower preserve and morella syrup. While the Count produces for the table a very highly spiced quince cheese, black and sticky, but very good.

The ravished vineyards are a sad sight on the brown earth of the property. The Count pauses from time to time in his passage between the kitchen and the dining-room terrace to contemplate them. He is happy with the full weight of his resignation: because October is coming with its first sweep of rain and mist. The remaining vine-leaves and fig-leaves—strange butterfly-like shapes against the massive platinum-grey trunks—will be gathered for fodder. The earth will die shabbily and dully in russet patches, tessellating the landscape with its red squares and octagons. In November the cleaning of guns, the first wood fires, and the putting away of summer clothes. Then the earth will spin inexorably into winter with its gales and storms—the wild duck screaming from Albania, the seas shrieking and whistling off the barren northern point beyond Turtle-Dove Island.

These few days pass in a calm so absolute, that to regret their passing would be unworthy of them. Zarian is bound for Geneva next week. Nimiec for Poland until next spring.

We picnic for supper on these warm nights by the Myrtiotissa monastery. Spiro lights a fire of pine-branches and twigs, and the three wicker hampers of the Count are brimmed with food and drink. In the immense volume of the sea's breathing our voices are restored to their true proportion—insignificant, small and shrill with a happiness this landscape allows us but does not notice. The firelight etches the faces so clearly. The Count with his bright eyes looking over N.'s shoulder as she draws. Theodore's golden beard lowered over a pool in complete abstraction. Nimiec and Caroline walking with linked fingers into the sea. Zarian's lips shiny with wine, his silver scruff of hair flying like a halo round his head. Spiro's great charred features. Everyone. The night around us edges slowly on towards the morning, silent except for the noise of the sea, and the sleepy chirp of cicadas in the plane-tree who have mistaken our fire for sunlight. 'You have noticed how we talk less and less together as the days go on,' says the Count. 'It is not because we have less to say to each other, it is because language becomes inadequate to our parting. I do not know when we shall meet again. Will you all be back by next spring I wonder?'

It is already very late, and the donkeys have stumbled off home with the hampers. Theodore lies asleep in the firelight. His lips move slowly. Zarian has taken the guitar from Bocklin and has started to play it inexpertly. He is trying to find the key for the little island song which Theodore has taught us.

> 'Sea, you youth-swallower,
> O poison-bearing element, Sea,
> Who make our island folk
> Always be wearing their black clothes.
>
> Have you not had enough of it,
> Sea, in all this long time,
> With the bodies you have swallowed
> Down in your insatiable waves?'

Presently Theodore will wake and ask Caroline to sing 'Green-sleeves' and 'Early One Morning'—airs sounding in all that emptiness so Lydian and remote coming from those American lips with their limping southern drawl.

To-morrow we are separating.

1.1.41

A postcard from the Count: 'Christmas Day. I spent it alone in happy memory of the year before when we walked across the northern marshes and you were attacked by a wounded hare— remember? To remind myself (and hence you also) of our per-petual spring I gathered a bunch of flowers from the valley—

The Vintage Time

flowers from every season. Cyclamen and snowdrop. February's irises and a jonquil, cinquefoil, bugloss, corn marigold, orange blossom, clover, and wild roses. Spiro has asked one of his pilots to fly them to you so you will have them by now. They are my invitation for next year. Don't forget us.'

VIII

Epilogue in Alexandria

The sightless Pharos turns its blind eye upon a coast, featureless, level and sandy. One thinks of Nelson on his column turning a blinded eye across the miles of English mist to where by the deserted gun batteries of Aboukir the sea runs thin and green. In these summer twilights the city lies in its jumble of pastel tones, faintly veined like an exhausted petal. Flocks of pigeons wheel in the last sunlight, turning and falling, like a shower of confetti when the light strikes against their wings. The last landmark on the edge of Africa. The battleships in their arrowed blackness turn slowly in the harbour. The loss of Greece has been an amputation. All Epictetus could not console one against it.

Here we miss Greece as a living body; a landscape lying up close against the sky, suspended on the blue lion-pads of mountains. And above all, we miss the Eye: for the summers of indolence and deduction on the northern beaches of our island—beaches incessantly washed and sponged by the green Ionian—taught us that Greece was not a country but a living eye. 'The Enormous Eye' Zarian used to call it. Walking in those valleys you knew with complete certainty that the traveller in this land could not record. It was rather as if he himself were recorded. The sensation of this immense hairless recording eye was everywhere; in the ringing blue sky, the temples, the supple brushes of cypress, the sun beating in a withering hypnotic dazzle on the statues with curly stone hair and blunt sagacious noses. Everything was the subject of the Eye. It was like a lens fitting into the groove of the horizon. Nowhere else has there ever been a landscape so aware of itself, conforming so marvellously to the dimensions of a human existence. At Epidaurus, for example, it is not the theatre that obsesses one or the temples, but the enfolding circle of small hills, as if the very land had conformed to the architect's plan: all contours, no edges, and only the faintest engraving of ilex and olive along the sky.

Epilogue in Alexandria

Something of all this lives on in the keen Athenian faces of our friends—faces so long turned towards the preoccupation of Greece that you can read everything in them: the dark uncombed blue of the Cyclades slowly uncurling about the flanks of Mykonos and Delos: the dazzling windmills and the grey springs. But they are here now like ghosts of the old lucid past in the aura of that enormous Eye—Stephan sailing his boat like a demon, half seas over in blue and gold; girls like Elie with dark slanting arms and long olive legs; the shaggy islanders in their coloured belts; caves echoing to the suck and swish of the water; the long rows of coloured caiques snubbing at anchor in the oilgrey waters of the port; the church bells ringing. Meeting them in these crooked streets one is struck by the potentiality of the drama which the Greeks this time have offered to the world. Maro, the human and beautiful, in her struggle against apathy; the drawn face of Eleftheria with its haunting eyes reading the last few lines of her great poem; the solemn face of Seferiades with its candour and purity ('we are the dying limb, withering on the body of the tree cut down'); Alecco, Spiro, Paul. In them the thousand and one images of that Greece of ours crystallize into pin-points of light: the book-lined room where the woman of Zante was read: the terrace with the figs and the sound of running water: Tinos where the red sails walk down the main street: Corinth with its vermin: Argos and Thebes with their retzina: Kalamata choked in vines: the warm scent of bruised sage on the Arcadian hills.

I think of them all in Africa, in this unfamiliar element, as subtropical men, defeated by a world where the black compromise is king. I see them daily recovering by their acts, their songs and poems, the whole defeated world of acts and thoughts, into a small private universe: a Greek universe. Inside that world, where the islands lie buried in smoke, where the cypresses spring from the tombs, they know that there is nothing to be said. There is simply patience to be exercised. Patience and endurance and love. Some of us have vanished from the picture; some have had their love converted into black bile by the misery they have witnessed. Nimiec died in an Athens night-club. Spiro died in his own vine-wreathed house. Theodore with British forces in Italy punctuates the silence by characteristic letters beginning 'Do you remember?'

Epilogue in Alexandria

Zarian is in Geneva. His silence is complete. Caroline, Mitsu, Rosemary, are in Cairo. The Count is somewhere in the mountains of Epirus—a philosopher with his pockets full of dynamite. Bocklin is on the Russian front. The white house has been bombed and the boats too. History with her painful and unexpected changes cannot be made to pity or remember; that is *our* function.

The day war was declared we stood on the balcony of the white house in a green rain falling straight down out of heaven on to the glassy floor of the lagoon; we were destroying papers and books, packing clothes, emptying cupboards, both absorbed in the inner heart of the dark crystal, and as yet not conscious of separation.

In April of 1941, as I lay on the pitch-dark deck of a caique nosing past Matapan towards Crete, I found myself thinking back to that green rain upon a white balcony, in the shadow of Albania; thinking of it with a regret so luxurious and so deep that it did not stir the emotions at all. Seen through the transforming lens of memory the past seemed so enchanted that even thought would be unworthy of it. We never speak of it, having escaped: the house in ruins, the little black cutter smashed. I think only that the shrine with the three black cypresses and the tiny rock-pool where we bathed must still be left. Visited by the lowland summer mists the trembling landscape must still lie throughout the long afternoons, glowing and altering like a Chinese water-colour where the light of the sky leaks in. But can all these hastily written pages ever re-create more than a fraction of it?

IX

Appendix for Travellers

KARAGHIOSIS
(see Chapter IV)

'C'est à Karakouche, ministre de Salah Edine, que revient l'honneur d'avoir fait édifier la Citadelle. Il proposa en 1176 la construction d'un château ou le sultan pourrait loger. . . . Karakouche, plus communément connu sous le nom de Karaguez, avait fait détruire les petites pyramides de Gizeh et de Sakkara et employait leurs pierres a bâtir les remparts des édifices. Il s'était rendu très impopulaire par les nombreuses véxations qu'il avait fait subir au peuple pour lui permettre de réaliser les travaux d'utilité publique qu'il avait en vue. C'est pourquoi certains, pour se venger, commencèrent a brandir des fantoches a son image, auxquels ils donnèrent son nom. Ainsi, Karaguez entrait dans le tourbillon d'une brillante carrière de pitre qui jusqu'aujourd'hui amuse les foules sur les place publiques.'— G. ZANANIRI, *l'Egypte et l'Equilibre du Levant au Moyen Age.*

SOME PEASANT REMEDIES IN COMMON USE AGAINST DISEASE

1. *For all Fevers.* Infusion of the plant called Pharmakouli (a type of Erythrea, perhaps E. Centaurea).
2. *Kidney Troubles.* Infusion of plantain leaves (Plantago coronopus).
3. *Earache.* The brown silk with which the pinna shell fixes itself to the ocean bed, is said by sailors to be excellent in cases of earache. The ear is plugged with the silk.
4. *Stings, Bites.* Garlic or onion applied to the wound.
5. *Scorpion Bite.* A living scorpion dissolved in a bottle of olive oil, provides a remedy against the bites of other scorpions. Lotion applied externally.

Appendix for Travellers

6. *Dysentery or Diarrhoea.* A small bottle of beetroot juice (about 50 cc.) is corked and placed in the heart of an uncooked loaf of bread. The bread is baked and the bottle removed. The medicine is drunk in small quantities on successive days until symptoms cease.

7. *Open Wounds.* Infusion of cypress-cones used to dress wounds.

8. *Malaria.* The efficacy of quinine is supposed to be increased if taken with a little urine from an unweaned baby.

9. *Open wounds.* Cobwebs or cigarette-tobacco used to stanch flow of blood.

10. *Coughs, Colds.* Infusion of mallow flower.

11. *Indigestion.* Infusion of mint leaves and flowers used for flatulence, indigestion and all minor stomach disorders; often mixed with infusion of orange blossom.

12. *Piles.* Water from boiled onions applied in the form of hot fomentations.

13. *Seasickness.* Suck a lemon.

14. *The Evil Eye.* Blue stone amulet, price 3 drachmae. Worn by all horses and most motor-cars.

15. *Werwolves.* Garlic fixes both werwolves and witches.

16. *Rats.* An excellent rat poison is made by pounding the centre of asphodel bulbs and mixing with a little ordinary cheese.

17. *Warts.* Rub on juice of milk-wort.

18. *Skin eruptions and sores.* Strong infusion of Sambucco nigra used for skin trouble. Applied as poultices.

19. *Hollow teeth.* Juice of cloves on cotton wool.

Many of these peasant remedies show medical knowledge. No. 18 is particularly effective in the case of autumn sores, which are prevalent in Corfu towards the end of the year.

SYNOPTIC HISTORY OF THE ISLAND OF CORFU
B.C.

734   Island colonized by Corinth. (Town probably at Analypsis, Canoni.)

434   First sea victory in Greek history over Corinth. Took place off Lefkimi.

432   Corinthians repelled once more.

Appendix for Travellers

413   Corfu helps Athens in second Sicilian invasion.

373   Corfu helped by Athens beats off the Spartans under Mnasippus, who is killed.

361   Civil wars.

303   Corfu sacked by Spartan Cleonymnus.

301   Corfu sacked by Agathocles, Tyrant of Sicily.

229   Corfu conquered by Demetrius the Pharian with his Illyrian freebooters.

229   Taken by the Romans without resistance. Remains a Roman colony until A.D. 337.

A.D.

445   Raided by Vandals.

562   Raided by Goths.

733   Corfu comes under Byzantine Empire of Leo the Isaurian.

933   Raiding Slav pirates repulsed. Forts built on the hill near the town from which the island is supposed to get its name.

1032   Corfu raided by Barbary pirates who are destroyed by the Byzantines.

1080   Corfu conquered by Robert Guiscard, King of Sicily.

1149   Retaken by Byzantines after long siege.

1185   Retaken by Sicilians.

1191   Retaken by Byzantines.

1199   Corfu raided and taken by Genoese under Vetrano.

1203   Retaken by Byzantines.

1205   Conquered by the Venetians, who are however driven out by Vetrano.

1206   Vetrano defeated by Venetians and hanged.

1214   Corfu seized by Michael Douca, Despot of Epirus, who builds Castle of St. Angelo at Paleocastrizza.

1259   Helen, daughter of Michael II, receives the island as a dowry on her marriage with Manfred of Sicily.

1266   Manfred killed in battle. Island seized by Philip Cinardo for himself.

1266   Cinardo murdered.

1267   Island passes to Charles D'Anjou, King of Sicily and Naples.

1286   Island raided by Villaraut.

1292   Island raided by Roger Doria.

1303   Island raided by Catalans under Roger de Flor.

Appendix for Travellers

1373   Island raided by Jacques de Baux.

1382-6   Island passes to Charles D'Anjou II, on whose death the Anjou dynasty ends. At this time the first Jews came to Corfu.

1386   Corfu asks Venetians to take over the island.

1403   Island raided by the Genoese.

1431   Turks under Ali Bey are repulsed.

1537   First great siege by the Turks; 25,000 land at Gouvia and ravage the island throughout August, failing however to take the town. Abandon island in September carrying off 20,000 hostages into slavery.

1571   Don Juan of Austria wins victory of Lepanto over Turks. 1,500 Corfiot sailors in the battle.

1577-9   Town-walls built.

1716   Second great Turkish siege; 33,000 Turks land at Gouvia and Ypso. Repulsed before the town with great slaughter by John Schulemberg, an Austrian general in Venetian employ.

1797   Corfu with Ionian islands taken by French.

1799   French driven out by mixed Russo-Turkish force.

1807   Corfu returned to French by Treaty of Tilsit.

1814   Ionian Islands taken over by British.

1864   Corfu ce ed to Greece.

1923   Shelled and occupied by Italians for two months.

1940   Italian attack on Greece. Corfu used as target ground for Italian Air Force. Town almost completely destroyed.

1941   April. Entry of Germans into Athens.

1944   Battle between Germans and Italians for possession of island. Latest reports indicate starvation rife; town badly damaged; Jews deported; but Church of St. Spiridion still standing.

'During the worst part of the shelling, when the inhabitants were ordered to take refuge in the stoutly built Italian school, a very large number preferred to trust in the Saint, and his Church was crowded with worshippers, who to-day claim yet another miracle; for while the Italian school and other refuges like it were hit repeatedly and demolished, the Church of St. Spiridion was untouched and those in it emerged unscathed. To-day it is still proudly standing (December 1945).'

Appendix for Travellers

PLACES TO SEE

Canoni, Gastouri, Paleocastrizza, Pantocratoras, Benitza.

THINGS TO VISIT

Churches of St. Spiridion and St. Theodora (the Cathedral).
Monasteries of Myrtiotissa, Paleocastrizza, Pantocratoras.
Byzantine Church of St. Jason and Sosipater.
Library of Venetian MSS. and rare first editions.
Mother of Gorgons—beautiful stone relief in Museum.
Two old forts.

FOR SURREALISTS

The Achilleion. A monstrous building surrounded by gimcrack sculptures and lovely gardens belonging to the late Kaiser.
The Theatre. Shadowing the final end of the Italian operatic sense.

FOR HUNTERS

Two brackish lakes, one in the north of the island and one in the south, called respectively Antiniotissa and Korissia.

DRINKS TO TRY

Ouzo (*Ούζο*). Aniseed drink, taken with water. Resembling Arabic
   zibib and French pernod. Fairly strong intoxicant.
Raki (*'Ρακὶ*). Distilled from raisins. Alcoholic.
Salepi (*Σαλέπι*). Tea made from bulbs. Excellent. Swamp orchis
   provides the bulbs.
Retsina (*Ρετσὶνα*). Resinated wine. Turpentine flavour. Very good
   with meals but not for solitary drinking or parties.
Mastika (*Μαστὶχα*). Mastic liquor.

DISHES TO EXPERIMENT WITH

Whitebait fried with lemon. Ask for 'Marides' (*Μαρὶδες*).
Pipe fish fried with rice. Ask for 'Vellanida' (*βελλανὶδα*).

Appendix for Travellers

Cuttle fish with sauce. Ask for 'soupya' (Σουπειά).

Octopus with sauce. Ask for 'Ochtapodi' (Χταπόδι).

Meat or mince cooked in vine leaves. Ask for 'Dolmades' (Ντολμάδες).

Ionian Meat Balls, highly spiced. Ask for 'Kephtaydes' (Κεφτέδες).

Macaroni Pie. Ask for 'Pastischada' (Παστιτσάδα).

Red Mullet grilled. Ask for 'Barbouni' (Μπαρπούνι).

Fried Egg-plant. Ask for 'Melitzanes' (Μελιτσάνες).

Spitted meat. Delicious. Ask for 'Souvlakhia' (Σουβλάκια).

Ionian Welsh Rarebit. Ask for 'Saganaki' (Σαγανάκι).

Roasted Pinna shells.

Sole. Ask for 'Glosa' (Γλῶσσα).

(Crayfish is called Astacos ("Αστακὸς').

SWEETS TO TRY

Sesame sweet. White flaky blocks made from sesame, honey, and crushed almonds. Ask for 'Halva' (Χαλβὰ).

Yaourti. A sort of junket of curdled milk sprinkled with cinnamon (Γιαούρτι).

Waffles. Ball-shaped waffles of flour with honey. Ask for 'Loukoumades' (Λουκουμάδες).

Zante nougat. Sweetmeat called mandolato.

Pasteli. An ordinary nougat.

Other sweetmeats: Trigono, Kadaïfi, Baklava, Galactobouri.

BEST VILLAGE FESTIVALS

Gastouri; Kastellani; Analypsis; Pantocratoras; Kassopi.

BEST LOCAL WINES ON THE MARKET

Provata red and white; Lavranos red; Theotoki white wine.

Excellent private cellars can be breached at Aphra, Lakones, and Ypso.

Brief Bibliography in English

Henry Jervis White-Jervis, *History of the island of Corfu and of the Republic of the Ionian Islands.*

S. Atkinson, *An Artist in Corfu* (1911).

Viscount Kirkwall, 'Four Years in the Ionian'.

William Goodisson, A.B., *A historical and topographical Essay upon the islands of Corfu, etc.* (1822).

D. T. Anstead, *The Ionian Islands* (1863).

Index

Index